River$ of
Wealth®

The Path to an Ocean of Abundance

Bobby Norrson

Norrson Media Group, Inc.

www.norrsonmedia.com

Published by:

Norrson Media Group, Inc. - Raleigh, North Carolina.

Published simultaneously in Canada.

Library of Congress Cataloging-in-Publication Data:

Norrson, Bobby, 1970 - Rivers of Wealth

The Path to an Ocean of Abundance

ISBN: 978-0-578-04073-8 (pbk.)

Business/Motivation – United States.

Library of Congress Control Number: **2009911029**

Author Photo by **Al Greaves**

Printed in the United States of America

10 9 8 7 6 5 4 3 2 1

Limit of Liability/Disclaimer of Warranty:

While the Publisher and the Author have used their best efforts in preparing this book for the marketplace, they make no representations or warranties with respect to the accuracy or completeness of the contents of this book and specifically disclaim any implied warranties of its merchantability or fitness for a particular purpose. No warranty may be created or extended by sales representatives or written sales material. The advice and strategies contained herein may not be suitable for your situation. You should consult with a professional where appropriate. Neither the Publisher nor the Author shall be liable for any loss of profit or any other commercial damages, including but not limited to special, incidental, consequential, or other damages.

Bobby's Statement:

Listen up Ladies and Gentlemen. This book is not written for you to go by 100%. It is an idea generator, something to get your brain working. It is not just motivation but a possible strong guide to get you going towards your goal of financial Freedom. The Rivers of wealth I talk about are rivers I have seen others use to become wealthy and ones that I am using to also become wealthy. Now the knowledge is going to be in your hands. Just don't take it verbatim, come up with your own formula and work it until you reach your goals. Get some professional help in your inner circle to assist you in making the right decisions. Create your own circumstances. Below is a list of people that I believe should be in your inner circle or at least on your team. These professionals are worth the money and will help you along the way:

Family Attorney	Tax Attorney
Business Attorney	Entrepreneur as a Mentor
Certified Public Accountant (CPA)	Personal Accountant
Investment Bankers	Mortgage Brokers
Real Estate Broker/Agents	

This book is just my story and opinions. Take what you can use and trash the rest.

Norrson
Media Group

"The entrepreneur builds an enterprise; the technician builds a job."

Michael Gerber

This book is also dedicated to ALL soldiers who protect and gave their lives for this great country called the United States of America.

THANK YOU!

U.S. Army NCO Creed

No one is more professional than I. I am a Noncommissioned Officer, a leader of soldiers. As a Noncommissioned Officer, I realize that I am a member of a time honored corps, which is known as "The Backbone of the Army". I am proud of the Corps of Noncommissioned Officers and will at all times conduct myself so as to bring credit upon the Corps, the Military Service and my country regardless of the situation in which I find myself. I will not use my grade or position to attain pleasure, profit, or personal safety.

Competence is my watchword. My two basic responsibilities will always be uppermost in my mind -- accomplishment of my mission and the welfare of my soldiers. I will strive to remain tactically and technically proficient. I am aware of my role as a Noncommissioned Officer. I will fulfill my responsibilities inherent in that role. All soldiers are entitled to outstanding leadership; I will provide that leadership. I know my soldiers and I will always place their needs above my own. I will communicate consistently with my soldiers and never leave them uninformed. I will be fair and impartial when recommending both rewards and punishment.

Officers of my unit will have maximum time to accomplish their duties; they will not have to accomplish mine. I will earn their respect and confidence as well as that of my soldiers. I will be loyal to those with whom I serve; seniors, peers, and subordinates alike. I will exercise initiative by taking appropriate action in the absence of orders. I will not compromise my integrity, nor my moral courage. I will not forget, nor will I allow my comrades to forget that we are professionals, Noncommissioned Officers, leaders!

Table of Contents

Norrson
Media Group

"If you have a task to perform and are vitally interested in it, excited and challenged by it, then you will exert maximum energy. But in the excitement, the pain of fatigue dissipates, and the exuberance of what you hope to achieve overcomes the weariness."

Jimmy Carter

Special Dedication
To my Favorite Uncle

I dedicate this book to my Uncle Ed Jones
Ed S. Jones - 1943-2005

Really, right now I do not feel like communicating with anyone. However, I have committed to opening up my world to help people break out of the financial chokehold so many of us find ourselves in. I have found enough strength to type on my laptop about how I am feeling today and why I do what I do to help people break free financially. About an hour ago today, January 9, 2005, my Uncle Ed Jones passed away in Seattle, WA. A very close friend, confidant and father figure; he was a fairly young man. Uncle Ed and I were much alike, entrepreneurs, optimist, we loved airplanes and flying. We shared a lot of the same visions and growing pains.

I really loved being around and talking with him. Please forgive me; everything is hard to put into words because this just happened. I feel that if I were trying to verbally speak this, I would break down and cry which might not be a bad thing since I have retreated to my place of peace, which is any place with airplanes around. Anyway, I am going to use this situation to help you. Today has strengthen my conviction to finish this book and help as many people as I can break the financial handcuffs that hold them back in life.

You see, although I am not handcuffed together financially anymore, the cuffs are still connected to both hands. I have just been able to break the links and move freely a little bit. Therefore, I still have some work to do to completely remove them from my wrists. I can provide for my family and my business is stable at this time, but I do not have the freedom to fly to Seattle, TODAY and RIGHT NOW.

If I jumped on a plane right now, so many other things would get backed up. I am basically a one-man show, bills would go unpaid. My operations would slow down and affect my customers. That is not the right way to handle business and your life. This is why I stress the fact that we need to have the financial freedom to be able to take off across the country at a moments notice for an emergency and have someone handle your day to day duties until you return.

That freedom is what I mean when I state that I still have the cuffs on, but they are not connected. My desire at this point today is to walk over to General Aviation. Charter a private jet and fly to Seattle to be there with my uncle, but I can not do that right now. Not yet at least, I thought I had more time. My whole family assumed he would recover from this disease. This just shows us again that tomorrow is not promised. You don't have to be in a position to charter a jet, but at least be in a position to pay for a plane ticket at a moments notice, even if it cost $800. You will need to have a few thousand dollars at your disposal to take care of things like that at any given time....PERIOD!

I always thought that my uncle would be around to see the growth of all of my business ventures and we would fly airplanes together, as he was also a pilot. Now he can only be with me in spirit. I really assumed he would pull out of the health situation he was in and things would be back to normal. I would have time to spend with him and him with me.

Not realizing that the last time I saw him in our home town of Savannah, GA would be the last time I would ever see him alive. The point I am trying to make is you don't have to be in my situation and should be doing everything in your power not to be in financial handcuffs. Because important life moments don't announce when they are coming, the "Curve Balls" of life just hits you right in the face. So, please work on putting yourself in a solid financial situation so when you need to move, you can. Do not allow the lack of money to be the reason you can not move in case of an emergency or death in your family.

Put yourself in a situation where your job can not hold you back and the lack of financial resources (MONEY) is not an issue. Yes, it will take time and the road will sometimes be hard, but push on my friends and you WILL succeed! If I had the financial resources truly at my disposal, instead of being tied to a 9 to 5 job; I would be on the first thing smoking to Seattle, WA. As a matter of fact, I would have been there before Uncle Ed passed. The moment I heard of him being ill and in the hospital, I would have purchased plane tickets and took my whole family to be by his side until he recovered. That is how important he was to me.

I hope you read this book and catch what I am trying to show you. It should be enough to get you started on the road to financial freedom. Remember, you are not promised tomorrow and time definitely waits on no one, so make the best of your today. As you have seen in 2008 and now in 2009, the economy takes no prisoners. The famous quote from my good friend Drew Solomon, *"Do for Self or Suffer the Consequences"*. Generations are depending on you to succeed. Leave a legacy for your children and their children. Now dig in and push forward! **I will see you at the TOP!**

Norrson
Media Group

"Genius is 1% inspiration and 99% perspiration. Accordingly a genius is often merely a talented person who has done all of his or her homework."

Thomas Edison

Shontaire & Kids

To Shontaire, the Queen....thanks for putting up with me and this process. You were there when there was nothing and I love you for that. Thanks for taking care of the household and not complaining while I chased this dream.

To Ashawn, Kiara, LaMonica, Sharice, Mone't and Josiah, you all dealt with me and my constant running around building this business. Thank you from the bottom of my heart. All that I do, I do to provide you with a better lifestyle than I had. I hope I have made you proud.

Norrson
Media Group

"Imagination is more important than knowledge. For knowledge is limited, whereas imagination embraces the entire world, stimulating progress, giving birth to evolution."

Albert Einstein

Family & Friends Acknowledgments

To my caring Mothers (Jean & Velma).

My Dad (Bobby Sr., the Zank).

My sisters Kim and Hanniyyah.

My brothers Corey, Brian and Jerry.

All of my Aunts (Margaret, Sarah, Ann and Sandra) and Uncles (Paul, Eddie and Robert) thank you for your support. I know to some of you I would seem totally crazy with my ideas, but you supported me anyway and I thank you for that.

To Grandma Annie Mae and Mildred, without you two, I would not even be here. Thanks for all your love and support.

To all of my cousins, nieces and nephews, read this book and every book I recommend and you will not only become wealthy in monetary terms, but spiritually, physically and mentally.

To those who supported me, thank you. You confirmed that what I was doing had substance.

To those who doubted me, thanks...you were and still are the fuel that drives me, keep it coming. Watch what I do next. ☺

Norrson
Media Group

"Live as if you were to die tomorrow. Learn as if you
were to live forever."

Mahatma Gandhi

Inner Circle Acknowledgements

To Greg, Brian, Danyale, Richard, Sharon, Byron, Drew, Rada, Rolando, Salla, Jamie & Ollie. You all are my rock, the ones I come to for advice and support. You all listen and supported my crazy ideas. You saw my vision when I disclosed it to you and never doubted me.

I appreciate each and every one of you. God sent each of you to me and I shall always treasure that blessing. We are doing this together and no one shall be left behind. Billions are still left to be made, so let's go get as much as we can....TOGETHER!

Norrson
Media Group

"Destiny is not a matter of chance; it is a matter of choice. It is not a thing to be waited for; it is a thing to be achieved."

Jeremy Kitson

Jiacom & Norrson Team Acknowledgements

Thank You, Thank You and Thank You!

To the entire Jiacom-Norrson Inc team, from the radio show to the communications company. I had the vision and you made it a reality. You guys actually carried out the mission after the goals were set. Without your part, these projects could have never happened. I look forward to the new media network and some very fun years ahead.

Thanks for all your support and most of all for believing in the dream of a young crazy serial entrepreneur. Most people would call me crazy, but you all saw the vision God had given to me and you continue to stand with me...THANK YOU.

I hope that I touched and affected your life for the good in some way.

With Love & Many Blessings,

Norrson
Media Group

"It is good to dream, but it is better to dream and work. Faith is mighty, but action with faith is mightier. Desiring is helpful, but work and desire are invincible."

Thomas Robert Gaines

Introduction

For the academics and skeptics, HERE ARE MY CREDENTIALS! I have been broke; I mean penniless, homeless and lost. Have you ever been there? I know first hand, exactly what it is like to have no money, no car, no-nothing! I have been through foreclosures, car repo's, negative bank balances, bad credit, bankruptcy twice and any other financial set back you can think of. I didn't rob Peter to pay Paul.....I robbed both Peter and Paul to EAT!

I know what poverty is and I am serious about stamping out as much of it as I can around the world. I have no college degree nor have I attended any of the big business schools and I am definitely not a socialite. I do however have over eight years of leadership and management experience from being in the US Army. I even served in a war and jumped out of a perfectly good airplane a time or two all before the age of 21. My college was the US Army forcing me to lead and my many life's obstacles.

I learned what I know and am STILL learning, from the trial and errors world of this thing called entrepreneurship. Oh and by the way; I founded and now run a national, legitimate, soon-to-be multi-million dollar corporation. I also have my own media network which will soon have over 300,000 plus members across the nation. I coach small businesses on how to tap into the increasing $500 Billion plus spending budget of our Federal Government. For $397 I can teach you how! To the skeptics, the *"teach you how"* part is a joke. I really do not want your negative energy in my seminars.

Okay...now let's get to the folks who really matter. For those of you who are at your wits end or who just need some practical guidance. I will open up my world so that hopefully you can gain something to help you in moving up out of your financial pit. Remember this, when you are at rock bottom, the only way to go is up! It is my daily hope and prayer that my straight forward ideas will help you change your life and thereby your family's life financially. I have been where you are and/or are about to be if you don't get a grip on your money! Like I said before, this book is written with a deep passion to help you as I sat on my isle of Patmos. Everyday I see people who need some kind of down to earth common sense guidance on where to start earning money. People want to know what to do to get out of the financial rat race of life.

Alright the mushy stuff is over, let's get down to business. Here is a simple money test for you. Watch the movies **"John Q"** and **"The Pursuit of Happiness"**. If you would be okay in Denzel's and Will's situation, you can put this book down. If you would be lost, hanging on by a string like them, you need to keep reading. To live in this world, you have to have disposable income or you will forever be caught up in the financial rat race. You should not always depend on someone else for your paycheck. Living from day to day, not being in control of your financial world is not healthy. This is not the way you should live your life in my opinion.

As I am finishing the final chapters of this book you're reading now in the year 2009, over 45 million American are still living in poverty or are homeless, just getting by and living from pay-check to almost pay-check. The price of everything is up but your paychecks. Let's not even talk about the price of gas. One group of people that sticks out to me, among all Americans, are the soldiers who are serving in IRAQ or Afghanistan. Especially the Reserve and

National Guard troops who are serving in those campaigns. These part-time soldiers left a civilian job only to make LESS monthly and their families are getting hammered financially!

As I stated earlier, I participated in the first gulf war (Desert Storm). As a soldier in the US Army 18th and 82nd Airborne Corps, I can not imagine the financial grief a lot of our troops are dealing with now. Is the military to blame for a soldier's financial hardships? The correct answer is No! Hear me out when I say this, it is not our military's fault, it is yours and it was mine. The reason I bring this up is to make this point. A lot of these Reservist and National Guard troops are catching hell financially because they have most likely been taken from a high paying job only to earn a lower pay. Some of these soldiers were making two or three times what they actually make as an active duty soldier.

The obligation to deploy paired with bad money planning on the soldiers part puts them and their family in trouble financially. This only happens, IF THEY HAVE NOT PROPERLY PREPARED FOR this life "Curve Ball". That is why I say it is not our military's fault. Our financial future and strength is OUR responsibility not the Government's. You should NEVER EVER leave that aspect of your life in anyone's hands but your own...PERIOD! That is what this book is about, preparing for life's financial curve ball that is coming. Life WILL slap you with some issues and challenges like being activated and deployed for years or cancer. How prepared you are to handle these "Curve Balls" will determine the success you have in life.

Some soldiers and their families have to actually go to food closets to get food which should not be the case. How can we really expect the troops to fight in a war and live if they are concerned about their finances and family back home? That's where having **Rivers of Wealth** come into play. Most people live from day to day and never see the "Financial Disaster" storm coming their way. Some people know a storm will come and simply ignore it by not preparing for it which is a huge mistake! You can take ACTION now and be prepared for the storm or you can sit back and become a victim of the storm...it is your choice. Just don't point a finger at anyone else but yourself if you choose to sit back and/or get caught sleeping on the job.

This book is not for everybody. It is for the people who are broke and desperate for some ideas about how to possibly turn their money problems around. It is for the ones who are willing to follow a plan of action (as long as it's legal) regardless of the pain it causes. Changing from your current BROKE status will be hard, sometimes very hard, but IT WILL BE WORTH IT in the long run. Business school did not get me to where I am today. Trial and error did. My goal is to show a possible way around the trial and error I had to go through and deal with. When you are broke, it affects your health and mental state. You go to sleep stressed with needing money on your mind and you wake up stressed with not having enough money on your mind.

Being stressed out financially affects your life; spiritually, mentally and physically. So it is essential that you become very financially healthy fast...PERIOD! Building wealth via a small business is the best path to take. Someone who has a part-time or full time business can get better tax breaks than someone who is just an employee. This alone will help you become financially secure because you will have more money to invest into different opportunities that come to you. Simply putting $150 a month for the next 15 to 20 years could make you very wealthy.

Getting rich quick never lasts, be patience and strategic in growing your money tree.

Don't believe the hype. There are a lot of people driving Benz's, BMW and Lexus who can not afford them. Most of them are just a paycheck away from financial disaster. Don't let this be you and if it is you, change your habits NOW and build real wealth before it is too late. Just to get you in the entrepreneurship game, Network Marketing, Real Estate Investing and Stocks/Mutual Funds are the three *"Rivers of Wealth"* I will concentrate on in this book because they are what I know. However, there are many more "Rivers of Wealth" you can pursue. The key is to just make sure you do your homework and research businesses before you commit to that particular River of Wealth. Everybody has ideas about what they think you should do, you just go with what you love and you will be just fine.

If you don't know what you want to do in business, read books on and about entrepreneurs. Learn from the books about businesses that started with zero and build strong profitable organizations. Subscribe to Entrepreneur and business focused magazines. I promise, as you begin to read these niche materials. I bet you'll find something you would like to do. Determine what you are passionate about and see if it can bring you wealth. It does not matter if you have a college degree or dropped out of school. You can learn and master anything in this world that you put your mind too. I sincerely hope you enjoy and learn from what I have put together for you.

See You at the TOP!

Norrson
Media Group

"Every time you state what you want or believe, you're the first to hear it. It's a message to both you and others about what you think is possible. Don't put a ceiling on yourself."

Oprah Winfrey

From the Author

I want to first thank you for taking the time out of your busy schedule to read this book. It is my prayer that after you read "Rivers of Wealth", your life will begin to instantly change. It is often said that the difference between successful and un-successful people is the knowledge that the successful people have, use and continue to seek throughout their lives.

It is my goal to get some important knowledge and know how into your brain, so that you may acquire all that you desire in life. I will be suggesting some awesome books to read in conjunction with this one and I guarantee that if you apply the principles and philosophies in all that I present to you, you and the generations that follow you will be successful **S**piritually, **M**entally, **P**hysically and **F**inancially.

I have lived from paycheck to paycheck, took those cold ass showers, drove broke down lemon cars, been bankrupt twice and let me tell you; if you don't already know, **IT SUCKS!** I wrote this book to tell people about a plan I have to make sure I never live that way again and hopefully to help you never live that way again or ever start living that way.

In this book, I will be talking about the *Rivers of Wealth* I have selected to create the future wealth for my family. These rivers I have successfully started to create should yield my businesses, my team and my family Millions, if not Billions of dollars for generations to come. I believe that my philosophy pertaining to having Rivers of Wealth is the best method for securing a strong financial future. These *RIVERS* could do the same for you, regardless of your current situation. What I will be talking about is not new. Folks have been making money using these methods for years. This is just my spin on the subject matter to hopefully make it easier for you to grasp.

The book is for those who don't understand the big words yet and who can not relate to the other authors who write about these methods. I am going to give it to you as plain as possible. You just have to apply the information and take action. I am on a mission to stamp out as much poverty as I possibly can. When I find something that can benefit people, I share it, regardless of if I am making money from it or not. I take pleasure in sharing my ideas and plans with you as I travel this road of Entrepreneurship. I know that there is room for all of us to partake in the world's wealth harvest. Therefore, I am here to help you become financially secure.

Some of the RIVERS I talk about might work for you and some won't. I want you to just keep trying to build your financial health until you find the right fit for you. The point is for you to do something and do something NOW! There are many other rivers to choose from. This book is written simply to get your mind working and your eyes open to spot and capitalize on them. The rivers discussed are also rivers that only require baby steps. Once you have really gotten your feet wet, you can then begin to really look for the big opportunities and take advantage of them.

I have been an Entrepreneur for as far back as I can remember and I can definitely tell you about some hurdles I have fell across which caused me to land directly on my face. The difference between other people and me is that I always got up after the fall. Sometimes it would take longer than normal, but I got up and came up with a new way to work my plan to turn my dreams into a reality. I simply refuse to quit, I desire financial security that bad.

I have always taken my God given visions and tried to make them a reality. At any given time, you could find me leading someone or a group of people in some big project I have thought of. Now, looking back, I see a lot of things I could have done differently only if I had some straight forward practical information and mentorship, but most importantly, practical information that I followed.

Thank God, I am still young and have recovered from my state of misunderstanding of the chess game of life and how to play it. Remember this, if you take nothing else from this book. Life is like a game of chess or checkers. You must understand the rules of the game in order to win. The better you understand the rules of the game, the better your chances are of creating winning strategies.

That's my strategy with federal contracting. I learned and now understand the rules, which will lead to millions of dollars for my small business. So, learn the rules and making the money will not be a problem. Having patience will be the challenge. Sometimes it takes years to get that first big check. I have been running my media firm; that is producing my radio show. I hosted it for over two years now and have not made a profit.

I have been spending my own money with the help of a few investors and that is it. However, we have created a plan that will generate thousands per month for the business and allow us to prepare to raise $1,000,000 in 2011. Between 2011 and 2013 we should be able to raise $5,000,000 in investment capital to grow my company. In 2012, we plan to do an Initial Public Offering (IPO). I started with ZERO! My point is success takes time, hang in there and be creative!

Later on in this book, you will learn how to leverage your job, if you so please and become truly financially independent at the same time. Let me say right off top what my position is on the topic of keeping or quitting your job. I am not here to tell you to quit your job or stay at your job if you have one. My goal is to give you a practical guide to use as a road map to gain financial freedom.

Some things I suggest in this book you will not be able use or even like to use. My friends: that will be just fine with me. Everything I speak about will not apply to you. Take out of this book what will help you and trash the rest. Use this book to get your mind turning on other possible ways to create your own **"Rivers of Wealth"**. Your financial future is YOUR responsibility and if you do not take charge of it NOW, no one else will!

This book is a way to get ideas about how to create "Rivers of Wealth" which are different avenues of income coming from more than one source. This you will need so that inflation, slow business and/or your employer won't affect your lifestyle with the ups and downs that <u>WILL</u> come. This book is about creating wealth and I know there are a lot of these types of books out there. I highly suggest you get your hands on everyone of them. Read them until you know them like the back of your hand.

Remember, creating "Rivers of Wealth" is a chess game and you must first understand the game and the rules to win big. I hope that my straight forward ideas will help you. Once again, this book was written with passion as I sat on my isle of Patmos. Everyday I see people who need just some kind of guidance as to where to start and what to do when it comes to building massive wealth.

We are in a world where there will only be the haves and the have nots. The year of 2009 has shown us that. The banks got the bailout money and are not lending it out. They got help and are ignoring you and me. The big corporations got bailout money and are having $300,000 parties. People are losing property like crazy. The value of most things is dropping.

The middle class is not so middle class anymore and are struggling from check to check just like those who live in poverty. To live in this world, you have to have disposable income or you will forever be caught up in the financial rat race. There is OPPORTUNITY out there. You just have to have your eyes open to see it. We will talk more about this in the coming chapters, so let's get started.

Some of you are scratching your head wondering what my Isle of Patmos is. I see you have not been really studying your bible. ☺ The Isle of Patmos is the Island where John the Baptist was banished to in Revelations 1:9 of the Holy Bible. Like John the Baptist, on my Isle of Patmos was being in debt and full of stress. I often received revelations from God concerning financial security and helping people. I can identify with you because I have experienced the same trails and tribulations you experience in life.

Norrson
Media Group

"Life without risks is not worth living."

Charles A. Lindbergh

Chapter 1

Successful by Default

"You are programmed for Success"

When you get a new computer, it usually has software already installed on it and sometimes you have to download new software depending on what you need your computer to do. Software for a new computer is a group of preset tools that will make your new computer run successfully. Have you ever noticed that after you downloaded some new software to your computer and after it finished installing itself, it informed you that the new software is not set as your default software?

Then it proceeds to ask you whether you would like to have the new software set as your default software. You answer yes or no and it is done according to your wishes. Default software is the software of choice. You use it on a regular basis and it is the preferred software for you. You know how to use it and it works for you naturally. You're successful with it and the software performs its task to the point every time you instruct it to do so.

Well, just as your computer has default settings, so do you. God made each one of us in his own image. God is the most successful being we know, I don't care how many times scientists try to prove him wrong. Therefore, you are Successful by Default. Failure is not your end unless you choose it. Your body's computer system is programmed to succeed. All you have to do is customize the default system installed in you by educating yourself and relentlessly pursue the talents you have been given.

God has already installed every software program in you that you will need to succeed. If you would just open them up and began to use them, your whole life; not just in the aspect of finances, will change for the better. You can do this if you choose to change. Abundance is what God Prayed you would have, not poverty, which is lack. Lack leads to confusion. God IS NOT a god of Confusion...Satan is...Period. Reboot your mental computer and let's go do some extraordinary things in this world!

Right now, your pockets have a lot of holes in them. Let's plug them, starting now. Then, we can start to think about nicer cars and homes and all that other great stuff that comes with being financially free. It is the great year of 2008, January actually and if you can not see that you have to take control of your own financial destiny now, I don't know what it will take to wake you up. You get up and go to work everyday...hating it.

Those companies, that our mom and dad said were good companies to work for, are laying people off like crazy. Last year alone, over 100,000 people in the once big mortgage industry lost their jobs due to the USA mortgage meltdown. The more machines and technology improve, the less time companies will need you and I. Most of these companies could care less about your mortgage, your car notes, the college tuition you have to pay or those braces on your child's teeth. OH..., did I forget about the student loans and the medical bills? How dare me!

Even the mortgage companies and major corporations are getting bailed out by our government because bankruptcy is knocking at their door too. The system is not designed to help you. You have to help YOU! The bottom line is company shareholders want better returns on their investments and more money. The goal is to achieve this with as few people as possible. So the easiest thing to do for a major corporation (small one's too!) is cut the human resources (YOU!). Don't get me wrong, I understand the process. I am a CEO too and have to watch where I am spending money and make cutbacks when needed in my business. I am trying not to over hire people, that way I don't have to lay anyone off. My team and I understand that we have to wear multiple hats in this day and age.

It is my job to keep costs low and revenue high and sometimes you have to make tough decisions. My point is don't let the check you get for your services from the company you work for, excuse me....the company you have an agreement with, be the only source of income coming into your household. If this is the case and it is not changed soon, you are setting yourself up for guaranteed failure!

We both know that inflation is rising faster than your current income. Really, have you taken a good look at the gas prices lately or the price of coffee, milk, food and utilities? The cost of everything is rising, but your paycheck just stays the same. Now here is the big QUESTION. What are YOU going to do about it? The pizza delivery guy thinks twice about delivering your pizza because he or she can't afford to pay for the gas required to keep his car on the road. Eating out or going to the movies is becoming a thing of the past. Mom is keeping that money to put in the gas tank. So, what else is there to do but create some additional wealth to insure the financial stability for yourself and your whole family?

I went into a grocery store the other day on purpose. I knew from reading the BUSINESS section of the local newspaper that this particular grocery chain was closing all their stores. Over 20,000 people were going to be out of jobs. My goal was to get a general idea of how the employees at the store, who mind you are about to lose their jobs, were feeling about the whole situation.

Just as I had imagined, those employees were not happy about the store closing and they just accepted the fact they were going to have to go out job hunting all over again. I am sure the managers of the store were setting themselves up with other jobs but I was talking to the baggers and cashiers...the ones, who have a serious burden to bear. I especially targeted the people that do not have any other type of income flowing into their bank accounts every month.

They were not hard to find. You could easily see who had a plan and who didn't. It showed on their faces very clear. All I would say is hello and how do you like working here? I would get the whole run down. I can not stress this enough. You have to have 2 or 3 Rivers of Wealth in this world today. Those streams should be from only one job and the rest from small businesses you have started, not a part-time job. If you need a part-time job, it should be temporary only, simply a means to an end.

Realistically this is not only happening at grocery store chains, it is happening at your big electric companies, banks, auto makers, the post office. You name it. Almost everyday, you can find some firm or corporation in the newspaper that is letting a few hundred or a few thousand people go. I know for a fact the United States Postmaster General asked Congress to release them from the obligation to fund the postal worker retirement fund to the tune of about $5 BILLION dollars! Now are you telling me you're safe at your GOOD job? Hmm...you are going to retire and live the good life...huh? ☺ So Mr. or Mrs. Smarty pants, tell me. Where is the retirement money going to come from if it is not being deposited into a retirement account?

Oh...your Union is going to protect you? Well, I was a Postal Union Steward. I even ran for President of my local union. I saw the politics first hand and fought for the rights of all employees. Don't get me wrong, unions can be great for employees. However, corporations never and I mean never sign a union contract with a union that does not leave them with a back door to head out of tight situations.

You might have a contract that says you can not be laid off. That does not mean they can not change your whole life around by abolishing your job and requiring you to move 500 miles away from your home. YOU ARE NOT SAFE! All a corporation has to do to get out of that contract they signed with your Union is file for bankruptcy protection. They will get rid of you and find someone willing to do the job for less and without benefits. This is not what I heard, this is what I know!

Although I would love to believe that all the folks who are getting the "Pink Slips" have another source of income, I'm guessing...THEY DON'T. These people have no other income and are one check away from being BROKE! They simply got caught sleeping at the financial security wheel when they should have been busy like a "fire-ant" securing their financial future. Just because you make $100K per year, doesn't mean you should have a $300K lifestyle. We Americans do that, assuming money will always be there. I know what I am talking about. I used to be just like that. Spending more money than I had, faking it until I made it.

There are a few guarantees in life and one of them is that life will deliver you some hard times. Life's hard financial "Curve balls" are what I like to call these moments. You think your world is great and everything is going smooth. Then WHAM! Out of nowhere all of a sudden, the transmission on your "Just Paid Off" car gives out....and the warranty has also just expired.

It is the end of September and your car A/C unit just quits. A new one will cost $5,000 to fix. A close relative passes and you spend the $700 you had "Saved" attending the services and visiting family. The good company you work for sells to or mergers with a larger corporation and they eliminate your position in December. You know you were going to skip that December mortgage payment and buy Christmas gifts. That is what Christmas is about right? Now you don't even have that December check. I will not even get into that subject, let's move on. You know the financial "Curve Ball" is coming, but you just can never really anticipate when it will come across the plate (Your Life). One day it will be at your door step and if you are not prepared to handle it or them; those hard times will hurt you financially and emotionally.

Even though it might not literally kill you, it could cause you to lose a lot of things you have worked so hard to gain. It will bring stress into your life and stress kills! So even if you have a $30K per year income, try to get into something LEGAL and increase that amount. Live off of that $30,000 and get another income source (a RIVER OF WEALTH) to gain financial security. It can be done. You just have to create a plan and then put serious relentless action to it. Wealth is not hard to build. It just takes a little time and persistence, so let's go get it! *If you Dream it, you can do it!*

You WIN and You WIN BIG

So, even if you're waist deep in the no money dirt, I mean really in a financial hardship ditch that you think you cannot get out of. I HAVE GREAT NEWS! You can still enter into and WIN the race of financial freedom. You were born to win. Your destiny has already been set in place, written in stone. Every one of us was put on this earth to do something great and that something is called fulfilling your Destiny. Now whether you choose to define and pursue your Destiny is another story. I am here to tell you that if you can **DREAM IT**, it can become a reality, no matter how crazy it sounds or seems. No matter where you are in life right now, make the decision and go for it! Awaken the warrior spirit within you. Release your passion and energy. Go forward and relentlessly pursue your dreams!

Every resource you will ever need is at your disposal. If you do not know anything about realizing your Destiny, go to the library or get on the Internet. Get a mentor or join a group specializing in what you are going to be doing. Learn how others reached their Destiny and then form your own formula on how to achieve yours. If you want to build rocket ships, you can. If you want to be a marine biologist or a dentist with your own practice, you can. If you want to become a Billionaire, YOU CAN! It is your choice. Choose to fulfill your Destiny and Live Your Dreams.

You choose whether to walk your Destiny out or not. So many people live in this world today in what I call "the quiet desperation". They want deeply to do and achieve more, but they allow life to dictate what they can and cannot do. Some people simply don't care to do anything. That is their choice. It is a dumb, lazy one in my opinion, but it's their choice.

I know where I live, $2,000 a month might get you a decent place to stay. You will need to have a spouse's income or have a roommate to add to that $2,000, if you don't want to struggle from check to check. I live between NC and GA. If you are single, not to mention a single parent, you have to make at least $55,000 per year to live a decent lifestyle. That will not include major trips or real vacations. So if you are making anything less than that, keep reading and I will show you a way out, if you really want out of that financial ditch you are in.

Look at our seniors in the US. Some of them can't even afford medical coverage nor do they have enough money for their prescriptions. That little retirement or social security check they get cannot even pay the mortgage or rent. How are they supposed to do anything else? Those seniors we observe working at Wal-Mart are not there because they want to be there, at least not most of them. I believe the majority of them are there to cover the financial demand of their constant bills. Why would anyone want to work into their golden years? ANSWER: They DON'T, but they HAVE TO! Do you want to be that person?

I know I come off as harsh to some, but I just can't understand why a perfectly healthy human, with great potential would not want to pursue his or her dreams of financial stability relentlessly. You know deep inside that you should but you don't, go figure! All I can say is that if the shoes fit, wear them. As you might see, I really hate. I know you are not supposed to hate. However, there are two things in this world that really get under my skin. They are a lazy complaining person and poverty. Being broke and miserable is NOT what God intended for you. YOU have to decide that you are going to change your life. If you have read this far, you are the type of person who desires more and you will get it if you keep taking baby steps.

Everything you need to succeed you already have within you. You are successful and you're truly successful by Default! The way I became successful was by studying other people who I considered to be successful. I studied those who the world recognized as successful. I especially studied those who the world said had failed. You can learn a lot from someone else's set backs. I learned by reading everything I could get my hands on. This gave me great instructions on what to watch out for and how to navigate the financial obstacles.

You do not have to re-invent the wheel. Just learn how financial stability was achieved and follow the plan with a little of your own twist. Everything I will talk about in this book has already been done. There are real people who have been very successful at doing these things, so why not you? Your brain is no different than theirs. You just might have to work a little harder, but it can be done. Look at Richard Branson, Oprah, Mark Burnett, Tyler Perry, Lance Armstrong, Tyra Banks, Robert Johnson, Jay Z, R. Donahue Peebles and the list goes on and on.

Let me stop and say this right now. This book is about financial freedom thru business ownership. However, you can do anything in life you want to do. How many people thought that Barack Obama could become the President of the United States when he first started? No one was even paying him any attention. **ANYTHING IS POSSIBLE**, even when your back is against the wall.

Here is a very simple solution for you to turn your life around. If you want to be a Millionaire, study all the

Millionaires you can find. Get their success formula and follow it to the end. The same applies to those of us who are reaching for the Billionaire level. With dignity and respect: Do what they do, speak like they speak, dress like they dress, READ what they read and you will have a great chance of becoming super wealthy just like them. Doing what I just prescribed gives you a better chance of really becoming a Millionaire or Billionaire than playing the lottery. Wishing on a star will not make you rich, a plan with **ACTION** will.

More people in the world would rather play the lottery than WORK at building wealth. Too many people in the world want everything quick and easy, but it just does not work that way for most. Quick and easy or instant gratification is disaster in disguise. That is how most people get caught up in schemes and then they want to blame it on the scheming person or firm when it really was their fault. If you were not looking for the quick buck, the schemer would never have a fighting chance with scheming you.

Okay, back to my prescription for success. Pick out some people who you admire and wouldn't mind being like. Then take what you really admired about them and put it into your personal success plan. Leave out the rest as it will not be of any good to you. For example, I have over 30 businesses that I will start some day. I needed to find some real life evidence of someone running multiple businesses. After some digging around, I found a guy name Richard Branson, he runs a little company call Virgin...maybe you've heard of him. This guy is the ultimate Entrepreneur, with multiple businesses. I think he has started over 300 to this day.

Anyway, I got everything I could on Richard Branson and his company Virgin. Just so happens, he wrote a few books;

I bought them and read them about 3 times each. I learned more about business from reading those books and it has helped me grow as a young Entrepreneur and CEO. What this taught me was I was not crazy like most would have me think. It also taught me that I could achieve this Dream because someone had already done it before. Just because you own multiple businesses does not mean you actually run the day to day operations of those businesses. There are plenty of people out here willing to do that for you. I didn't even have to spend four years in business school for it. I got the books for about $20 or $30 bucks and some people pay hundreds of thousands of dollars for this information to be taught to them. Hey Thanks Richard!

I also studied Jack Welch, who ran GE and is a master at launching and growing businesses. I studied Bob Johnson of BET and the Charlotte Bobcats, (Hope to have those court-side seats one day) Mary Kay, Jim Goodnight, Mark Burnett and a host of others. Mark Burnett's book..."JUMP IN" is great. "JUMP IN" is a must read. I highly, highly recommend it as a part of your reading library. Another great person to study is Warren Buffet. He is a very smart man. I personally branded him the Take-Over-King. He sees opportunity and takes advantage of it.

When I was growing up in Savannah, GA, no one ever told me to study successful people. We just concentrated on sports and trying to get a college scholarship. No one talked to us about becoming Entrepreneurs or starting a business. If we brought home low grades, we would hear about it from our family. Sometimes even get disciplined for bringing home low school grades. I never remember getting disciplined for not wanting to be in business for myself. Now, that I am much older and a little wiser, I can trace back to my fascination with airplanes. As far back as I can remember, I would always stop in my tracks at the sight or sound of an airplane. Today, I still find myself stopping when I hear or see an airplane.

The love of planes is the reason I decided to go into the aviation field of business. It is also the reason I am getting my private pilot license. My point is, when I was young, I did not communicate my love for planes and no one ever noticed how much I liked planes. Maybe, if I would have had traits of studying successful people and things, my energies would have been focused that way. I could have gone into the Army to fly jets instead of being in Logistics.

That's why you have to discover your dream and pursue it early in life. Figure out what you love, make a plan and pursue it. As parents, we have to look out for these signs in our children. We need to spend just as much time showing them how not to be slaves to money as we spend telling them to get good grades and a scholarship. Teach them to get the scholarships but don't allow them to think that debt is okay. Debt will require them to most likely have to work for someone else instead of doing what they really love.

With technology, our kids are in the perfect position to be successful Entrepreneurs if we as parents recognize and nourish their God given talents. Let that teenage boy have a Lawn Care business. Allow your daughter to do hair or start her own clothing line. This is going to help you also. You won't be spending thousands helping them out of situations. You won't be mortgaging your home to finance their dreams. They will be wealthy; it can get done on their own. You just have to give them the tools to work with. The sooner they start, the better off they will be in life.

Studying and researching will be the bulk of the work in your success plan. You need to learn how other successful people got to where they are in life. Then, you repeat the process while at the same time refining it to custom fit your life. Let me give you another example of how things could have been different if I had done what I am telling you about now. I am also a filmmaker. If I had been given advice early on and acted on it, like what I am giving you in this book, I could possibly have been able to finance my own films and signed a major deal by now. I was ready to make films over 10 years ago. However, most of my time was spent chasing the dollar.

I have seen movies come to the silver screen with the same ideas that I have had and they were highly successful. Being in a strong financial position to do the things in life you really desire is essential. It is essential not only for the things you desire personally. It is also essential to achieve your passions in life and for other reasons also, like to support your favorite charity. Having a basic regular job, living from paycheck to almost paycheck, just won't get it and you know it just as well as I do.

Opportunities are Abundant

If you want to become financially successful, there are millions of perfectly legal, upstanding, great opportunities out there in the world to choose from. The key is finding the thing or things you like and moving on them. Most people find really great opportunities everyday. The problem is they get started and don't follow through. You have to be persistent in business or you will never succeed. Even though I am a strong advocate for direct selling/network marketing as an initial launch into business, you definitely don't have to start there.

Some of you might have all the financial resources you need to start a restaurant or computer service business. I personally know a guy who had two NFL football players at his disposal but he failed to use them as resources and ultimately lost out on potentially lucrative deals. Learn what you need to know, use the resources at your disposal and follow through.

There are State and Federal contracts to pursue, daycare businesses, printing and consultant businesses to start. You name it and with the right niche, you could create serious additional income from virtually anything. You can sell products and services on ebay and other sites like that. You just have to spend the time looking at any and everything and you will find something to get started with. Keep in mind that you should always have more than one income coming into your household. Remember what I coined as "Rivers of Wealth". Will you have to sacrifice some family time? YES!

I would rather spend three or four years building wealth and have the rest of my life to spend with my family. If you don't have financial resources, you are not going to have a very happy life. Somebody is going to get the short end of the stick. You and your spouse, if you have one, will have to work together as a team and you will be just fine. If you are single, then you can make more moves. Only work on the business two weekends out of the month instead of four. I only allow one weekend of the month for speaking engagements. Fridays and Sundays are usually my off days. I take the family out or we watch movies. I also cut my business lines to my phones off after 7pm daily. People still call me, but they do not get return calls until the next business day. You can offer me $50,000 and if it is not within the time I set, I will not be speaking. It is all about balance and the sooner you get into that routine, the better. Go ahead and determine and set the standard now.

Family time is important, but wealth is too. Don't make spending time with your family an excuse for not building a business and therefore creating wealth. Your family and generations that follow will honor you for your sacrifices. Do you think Richard Branson's kids are mad he spent a lot of his time building his businesses? Remember, it is all about life balance. Work on it everyday and everybody should be happy. If you don't have financial security, nobody will be happy. Lack creates stress and it is down hill from there, your choice!

Money Galore

There is a saying, *"It takes money to make money"*. In part that is true, but you first need the DESIRE to make the money in order to get to the people with the money. I know from first-hand experience that you can have no money one day and have $25,000 in your bank account the next day. The funds are out there. Where and how you get them will be the challenge. It is a challenge that you can rise above and the chase is so much fun! Some people choose to seek out investors and others try working two or three jobs to keep the business and the household up and running. I have done both and they both work. I like making my own money and then investing it into my business more than seeking multiple investors.

When you fund (finance) your business out of your own pocket, it is sometimes called "Shoestring Budgeting" or "Bootstrapping". Once again, I think bootstrapping is one of the best ways to start and grow a small business. For most of you, this will be the way you will have to grow your business. Most people think they can just write a business plan and go straight to the bank and get a loan or a credit line. There are people, who can just go to the bank and get a loan or a credit line. However, they already have the money and/or collateral to cover that loan or credit line. The loan officer still chooses whether or not they should do business with you. Banks are safe and have a fiduciary responsibility to protect our money, so your business will need to be very predictable and solid to get access to that money. Banks only like to loan to folks who already have the money. I never saw the logic in that.

Also, your personal and business credit will have to be very good to get a loan. This is not to scare you away from banks. I am in the process of getting my firms I's dotted and T's crossed for a possible loan or credit line application. I have to, because one of my businesses growth plan calls for a bank loan, credit line and/or Investors. If the plan did not call for it, I would not even think about applying for a loan or selling stock in my company. Just as it is good for you to carry as little debt as possible in your personal life, it is the same in business. The less debt you have, the better off you are. Do not allow someone to trick you into taking on more debt than you or your business really needs too, if any debt at all! That is why in 2009, we are in the financial situation we are all in now.

If you choose to secure financing via outside investors, make sure you have everything in writing. You need to get everything on paper to protect yourself and your business. There is nothing wrong with getting potential investors or anyone who can run with your ideas to sign a Non-Disclosure Agreement (NDA) before you go over the details of your business plan with them. If they have a problem with the NDA, don't do business with them.

Believe me, you can bring in an investor and everything will seem fine until that person who invested money in your business hits rocky times financially. When this happens, your phone will be ringing off the hook. They will be looking to get their money back or trying to get you to do any and everything to bring a quick return. Their motivation for doing this will be to get out of the mess THEY got themselves into. When you talk to potential investors and they tell you they are looking for a quick return, run and DO NOT do business with them. Real investments take time and NOTHING is guaranteed but death and taxes!

People change with the wind. Rarely do you find someone to work with you through thick and thin. Make them earn your trust via hard work and commitment. I have had a lot of people excited about what I was doing and the vision, only to have them waste weeks of my time and energy which is extremely valuable.

If you have it all on paper, this will not be an issue. When an issue arises, you can refer them to the legal agreements and keep growing your business. Remember, this is business and watch who you get close to. Things WILL go wrong and predictions will not line up the way you hope they might. That is why you make sure your investors understand the risk involved in your business before they hand over a check. The less investors in your business, the better it is for your business.

Keep your dealings with Investor 90% business and 10% personal and you will do fine in business. Remember people change and attitudes change. When a person has their back against the wall, it is no telling what they will do. When problems arise for Investors, most of the time they will only be looking out for themselves. Seek outside Investors carefully and take the time necessary to choose them. Find out what they really want to get out of the deal and PUT IT ON PAPER!

People Galore

You will need a team and resources even more than money to accomplish your dreams. You may be able to get to a certain point on your own good looks. ☺ However, in order to really become successful; you will have to have a support team. Without a good support team, your new business will just drag along, never really gaining any speed. Find folks with great attitudes and train them for skill. You might find someone who is not an accountant, but is willing to learn and truly believes in your vision. Bring them on board and train them to become an accountant. Be mindful, this person should already be pursuing the certifications in the field. Check to see if they have signed up for or taken any real accounting classes. If they have, they are serious. If they have no plans of taking accounting classes, don't let them near your books. If they say they want to work in your marketing department, the same rules apply.

Always choose based on character first and skill second. There are some highly qualified folks out there in the world but their attitudes are terrible. The last thing you want on your team is a negative spirit. One bad apple does really spoil the whole bunch. Don't rush to get them in business with you. Go out golfing or bowling with them. This is a good way to really see who they are. Watch their reaction when they don't hit the ball as far as they like or when they don't get the strike they were hoping for. If they react like a spoiled brat, they will do that when times get hard in business and might be a rotten apple. If they are calm and excited about trying again, you might have a winner on your hands. Always look for the potential in people.

You are going to have to get out and network in order to meet people. They will not fall into your lap. A lot of my key Executives are people whom I have either met at different places or were referrals. Time will get rid of the folks who THINK they want to be on your team. As soon as they see that what they thought was going to happen, in the time THEY needed it to happen, is not going to happen they will move on. I sometimes make the mistake of getting excited about someone too fast and they turn out not to be the right fit for my business. People can fake it for a while, so don't think twice about firing them when you see their true colors.

You should be able to count your closest friends on one hand. Everybody else is associates. Your core Executive team should not consist of more than 12 people. You should be on a personal and business level with them. Personally, meaning you can visit for birthdays, cookouts and weddings, etc.; but in business, they do not have an issue with following your leadership. They understand that you are in charge. If it is not like that, remove them from your core team ASAP!

Stop Procrastinating

Procrastination is the great killer of all dreams. The world knows this, yet we still allow it to control our lives...WHY! Well my friend, I will tell you why. FEAR...fear that you will succeed. I get caught every now and then. I put this book down afraid no one would really like or read it. Then, the reminder comes with the hurricanes in New Orleans and in Texas. They make me say....I have to stop procrastinating and get this book out, so people can see the options you have available to them.

So...Bobby, how can I stop procrastination? I say, LOOK AT YOUR LIFE! If you're broke as a joke and you see the craziness going on around you, you also will see that the little check you get from your job WILL NOT cut it. You need some serious extra income and a second job is not the answer!

If you are my age, you see that it seems as if time moves just a little faster than normal. It seems that there is never enough time in a day to accomplish what you need to get done. Listen folks, in order to become financially secure, it has to become a life changing event. You can not waste time in this process or you will be left behind. If you choose not to become financially free, your life will be full of lack, stress and depression. You choose, enough said!

Requirements for Success

Assuming you choose financial freedom, you will need a system overhaul. You have to see yourself as being successful first. How you think of yourself will affect and determine how others think of and see you. You are successful, walk in it, live in it. Make it happen!

READING AND LISTENING to motivational and inspirational CD/DVDs is a must. You have to read if you plan to become successful. Every road map has pretty much been put in a book. If you would just change your lifestyle and read, you would get to the finish line so much sooner. You will also be a lot wealthier. Get cable T.V. and write some of it off as a business expense. You should faithfully watch shows like "The Big Idea with Donny Dutch", "Shark Tank" and CSNBC. Any show talking about wealth building should be watched by you.

Here is a "Special Note" to my black brothers and sisters. It is said that if you want to hide anything from a Black/African American person, put it in a book. **THAT**

<u>**HAS TO CHANGE!**</u> If you are a Black American and want to enjoy the success already built in you, changes have to be made. Our race will have the spending power in the Trillions of dollars by the year 2012. Don't let that money miss your business. Everybody else READ MORE! Cut back on the romance novels ladies, turn off the sports channel men (except for the shows mentioned) and get your kids from in front of the TV also. If we take some of that time and spend it educating ourselves and growing a small business, life could be much better for all of us.

Now listen, I don't want you to go cold turkey, just carve out an hour or two and put reading or a business/personal development audio into the slot to grow your mind. This will make a very big difference in your life. Guys, if we learn business like we know sports, wealth building would be so easy. Learn the stats in a business or the stock market like you know the stats of your favorite team. Take that $600 or $1000 you use to go to the game and put that into your business, so one day you can own box seats at the stadium. Get your hair done twice a month instead of every week. These small changes can make a huge difference in your life now and later.

The Obstacles

This world is set up like a chess game, it is all strategies, moves and counter moves. You have to know the game in order to compete and WIN. I would say that Nay-Sayers would be an obstacle, but that is only if you allow them to be. I try not to waste one second with a negative person. I prefer not to even be in their area or space. Negative things and people are like an invisible cancer. If it is not positive, move away from it and if it is not lifting you up, get away from it...point blank!

People are going to always give you every reason something won't work. Rarely do they encourage you to go for it. My Aunt Margaret, who is a Pastor in Atlanta, GA, (God Bless her soul), encourages me whenever I come to her with a new idea or way to accomplish my goals. You need people like that in your corner because times will get hard and you will want to quit. That is when the encourager will step in and help you hang on. Thanks Auntie Margaret! Even when my mother Jean, would see something on TV that she thinks will help me in my business, she will call and tell me about it. That is the kind of support you need from family.

Money initially will be an obstacle but there are ways around that. I really believe that if you are broke with a job and sinking in debt, you can still make it. Don't go get a part time job, get in a good Direct Selling company. If you are not really comfortable with direct sales, then you're really not ready to get ahead. The reason I say this is because another job is just going to tax you more and take more time away from you and your family if you have one.

You don't have enough money to start a business from scratch or buy into a franchise…so what is your other option. The Direct Selling industry, also known as Network Marketing, provides opportunities for you that do not cost a lot to get started and the pay is based on YOUR efforts. If you don't have the money to get with a Direct Selling company, borrow it! We will talk about this industry in more detail in another chapter.

Another option I like if you are really broke is to start selling something on eBay, save and then grow from there. You have some stuff you can sell and make some money off of. If you don't have something to sell, offer to clean someone's garage in exchange to keep what you want and then sell it on Ebay.

The bottom line is you have to get into business and start making that money work for you. If you have a hundred dollars or more you could tap into a small business right now. Look into changing your Federal deductions. There is a way...READ, READ and READ. For example, while writing this book, I worked for the Postal Service. To get extra cash in my check, I increased my Federal deductions and had basically no Federal taxes coming out of my check. I will still have to pay taxes at the end of the year, but at least I have that money to get something going verses waiting to get it back from our great IRS at the end of the year with no profit at all. I use that $200 plus dollars to fund and grow my small business. Remember, I said you have to be strategic.

The Results

I know a lot of you are turned away from some or all of my strategies and if you are...I hope your plan works for you. For those who really don't care for my strategies, HELLO!.....it is not about what you like right now, it is about legally generating money to do what you really want to do later. Listen, you have to start somewhere and we have already determined that you do not have the money to launch your dream business or buy into a franchise. Other options are coming later, just continue to read.

I didn't like getting up going to the post office to work everyday, but it allowed me to be able to keep my family fed while I was building my businesses. It allowed me to buy Real Estate and put money into my household and business. The best thing out of all of that is that I knew that everyday I went to that post office was my last day going to that post office and I relaxed in that. The result will be, total success, not only financially, but Spiritually, Mentally and Physically.

If you can dream it, buddy it can be done!

IMAGINE THIS:

On a hot, July, Sunday afternoon, you are driving down the highway on your way to the grocery store. Your kids are in the car and you guys are all singing along to your favorite song. All of a sudden, you hear a noise and then you see smoke coming from the hood of your car. By the way, the car is a 1995 model with a cracked windshield and a jammed driver's door. You manage to get the car over to the side of the road to see what is wrong on the hot summer day.

You discover it has to be something with the car radiator. The car cannot move and it is your only car. Life has pitched a curve ball at you. Okay, what options do you have? Will you be able to have your car towed to a repair shop to be fixed and have the funds to get a rental car until the work is done?

If the problem happens to be a water pump, which can run $500 easily, can you afford to have it fixed on the spot? How long can you afford to keep your rental car if you can even get a rental car? What happens if you cannot do either and you have a full time job to go to? This is not to try and scare you. I just would like you to think about all the small things that can cripple you if you are not financially stable.

The ideal situation would be to have the funds to rent a car. Better yet, have a second or third car to use while your first car is being repaired. A regular job is not going to cut it. I was in that situation more than once and although I had a few friends I could call on, it still made me feel like less than a man when I was in that position. Every time this happened, I fussed and cursed and then dug in and continued to build my company. I knew that it would one day yield me and everyone involved with great returns. Now when a vehicle of mine needs fixing, I have two more to use in the mean time.

Look at your current situation like a big field with seeds in the ground. If you continue to work on it, one day you will look up and have a whole field to harvest and the hard efforts you put in would have been worth it. In closing, remember this, if you don't keep anything else I say in this book. If you are not ready to change your financial destiny and have to be talked into it, you will not make it. There has to be a burning desire down in your heart to change your life for the better.

The great news is that everything you need is in place waiting for you to take hold of it. After reading this chapter, I would like for you to write down all your dreams, hopes and desires. Don't tell anyone about them, just write them down and wait until you finish this book to pursue them.

YOU WILL WIN, BECAUSE YOU ARE SUCCESSFUL BY DEFAULT!

Norrson
Media Group

"Ability is what you're capable of doing. Motivation determines what you do. Attitude determines how well you do it."

Lou Holtz

Chapter 2

Straight Up, No Chaser

"Let's Make the Big Change"

The Past is the Past

Regardless of whether you were or are homeless, bankrupt or penniless, you were born to win. Your destiny has already been set in place. It is written in stone. You choose whether to walk it out or not. Everything you need to succeed, you already have. You are successful and you're successful by default! So let's get rid of all those negative thoughts and habits of the past. Let's make a new better financial world for your life.

So many people never move forward because they will not let go of the past. Don't get me wrong, you need to remember your past experiences to shape a better future. The past is your measuring stick to gauge what you will and will not tolerate or do. I can not forget that I came out of poverty, so I choose to move toward abundance. You have to do the same. Don't dwell on the past, learn from it and move on.

Baby Step Actions (BSA)

Remember the saying Rome was not built in a day? That saying hold true in your life as well. That means your life is not going to change overnight. Building wealth will take time and just because you think or plan for something to happen at a certain time, does not mean that it will happen in that time. Success in any endeavor takes time. The good news is that if you DREAM, PURSUE and NEVER QUIT. That which you have dreamed will manifest one day. You cannot make this happen by taking a pill.

Everybody wants it NOW and it just does not work that way. Time, determination and persistence are what will get you there, so don't quit your job just yet. If you don't have a job right now, get one! This will take care of the household while you create your Rivers of Wealth. It might be something you don't really like, but hang in there until you get your feet under yourself and you will be glad you did.

Here is why I say keep or get a job for now. First, the health care plan that comes with the job. The job will be covering your medical and dental issues. That will be one thing you don't have to worry about while building the "Rivers of Wealth". Second is your money which is now being well spent. Your current household bills are covered and then you have the freedom to invest into your business. You will not be under any real pressure to do a deal or do something unethical. You will be able to take the time necessary to ask the hard questions and make the right important decisions, when it comes to business.

Early on, one of the worst mistakes I made was to quit my jobs too soon. I would do this without having built my business to the point where it could pay my salary. If I was smart back then, I would have made sure I had at least 6 months of living expenses along with some cash flow to cover me and my family while I was out growing my business. Now looking back at everything else in my past, I really needed over $50,000 in reserve just to survive.

You see, in any business, you will need some Seed Capital and we will talk about that later. Basically, this is money to carry your business while you are out there building the business. Early on in business, the only thing you are really doing is burning through that seed capital or cash. You will hear a lot of people talk about bootstrapping the business and that is fine and dandy. At least until bootstrapping does not cover the bills of the business. So, having a job will help you in the process.

So keep the day or night job for now, but remember it is ONLY temporary. This way, the money your new business does generate can be re-invested back into the business to make it even bigger and better. Don't believe that hype. The majority of young CEO's or Entrepreneurs still have their day jobs and a lot less stress. Also, I would need to note, that these individuals don't see what everyone else calls a job as that. They view it as a contract for their time between them and a customer for professional services. I will give you exact strategies later. Think big and grow that business.

Knowledge is the Key

You can have all the money in the world but if you're stupid (uneducated) with it, there is a great chance you're going to do something dumb and lose it all. You may lose the money from being sued all the time. Do I really have to give examples? If you do not read and change your inner circle into a positive one, you will fail at almost anything you do. Well let's put it this way, you are not going to be successful at anything for long by putting the wrong people in your inner circle. Everything you need to know in this world to become financially successful is in a great deal of books. There are books out there that will give you a step by step guide on building wealth.

The knowledge you gain from reading these books will propel you and your businesses up to the next level. It is an absolute must that you read books on finances and wealth building in order to become financially successful. If you are homeless or can not afford to buy all the books listed or some new book you would like to read, get a LIBRARY card. Check the books out, they are FREE! Nine times out of ten, if it is not in the library, they can order it for you. Again, the best thing about this is that it is all FREE! So, there is no excuse on why you can not gain the knowledge you need to succeed.

The books you pick up might seem too big or boring. Remember this please my fellow current and future Entrepreneurs. The boring book you read might contain the exact formula you need to become financially free. Now ask yourself, is it worth the time? If more people associated reading with pleasure instead of pain, we would be better off financially in the world today.

The $12 Million Mistake

I remember reading about a guy who gave away $6 million dollars. He did this out of the kindness of his heart and based on his faith. What he got was a lot of debt from failed businesses and creditors calling him all the time. Had he read one of those boring books that we seem to hate, he might have picked up a tip of information on how to live off the INTEREST of the $12 million. This way, he would have never gone broke.

Just getting 7% on $12 million in the bank would have given him about $70,000 to play with every single month. He still could have donated money and had plenty to live off of. How would you like to have $70,000 per month for life?

My point to you is to make a lot of money and base your lifestyle on the INTEREST it generates for you. This will ensure that the generations that follow you will have a head start in a world that it takes money to operate in. Now here is a good tip on how NOT to blow your money on books, tapes and newsletter programs.

There are a lot of people selling INFORMATION, just as I am, on TV. However, they are not selling the whole truth. We all have seen the programs at least once or twice, some even more. Millions have bought these products and later found out that they have been scammed. When you see something on TV, it is called an infomercial and its sole purpose is to sell you a product or service, in most cases, not to help you. I call these people the great persuaders. They are great actors and their sole mission is to sell you as many books or tapes as possible. I want to sell as many books as possible too, but I want them to help you also. Some of the material helps don't get me wrong. Once again, more than less, they are there to get you hooked. You could go to the library and get the same information for FREE!

Here is how to determine if the person that is trying to sell you something is worth the money. Get on the Internet and type their name in a search engine and see what comes up. If they have a lot of bad reviews or complaints against them, DON"T BUY THEIR PRODUCT! There are websites such as skeptic.com and salon.com that will post information on scammers. The FTC has complaint pages you can review also. You have to do your research and try not to buy on impulse. Record the infomercial and do the research on your own. Then, if you still desire to buy the product or service then go right ahead. The important thing is to do your homework.

Here is an example of what I did when I saw an infomercial on something I was really interested in learning more about. I recorded the show and listened for key words because the person will not tell you everything because they want you to buy the product. That's how they make money. Anyway, this particular topic was on buying tax liens which is something we will talk about in a later chapter.

The infomercial personality was selling his product package for $39.95 plus shipping and handling. So this could have cost me about $40 or $50 bucks. That is not really bad for some good information. Instead of picking up the phone and ordering the product right away on impulse, I jumped on the Internet and typed in the words "buying tax liens". I found some great information on the topic for FREE! I read up on the subject and found a book written by a tax attorney for $17.00 at the book store. I know I have read the book at least three times. Now I understand the subject enough to buy Tax Liens and it is one of my growing "Rivers of Wealth".

What happened here? Well, first I got what I needed without spending as much money as the infomercial wanted me too. I learned more and got it faster by doing my own research. What the guy was talking about was pretty much true but he is in business like anyone else to sell his product. You have to listen and determine whether his product is worth the cost. I also did not see as many bad comments about his marketing and selling techniques.

This guy was talking about something he knew and did for a living. Some of these other guys know that there are people out there who are desperate and they prey on that. They know that if desperate people see something on T.V. that looks good. They will pull out their credit cards and not think twice about spending money right then. That is what these PURSADERS are banking on.

Remember, I talked about those folks who always get scammed. It is mostly their own fault and it is too late after the fact for them to try and get their money back because they most likely won't. There are guys out there telling you that you can eliminate your debt overnight...PLEASE! You did not get in your financial mess overnight. Therefore, you will not get out of your financial mess overnight...legally. There are people saying that the government will give you money to pay your bills. Yep...there are federal assistance programs out there with money to spend. However, you are not going to just pick up the phone and get money just like that. You will be filling out a whole lot of forms and jumping through a lot of hoops to get to that money. It is possible, but NOT as easy as these so-called marketing gurus say it is.

I was telling a friend about selling her products to the federal government and how she could become a multi-millionaire in the process. She replied to me saying, "Bobby you make it sound so easy, we have got to jump on this". I instantly said to her, that it was only easy after you have done your RESEARCH and understood the process; the Federal Chess Game. The government does have Billions to give away and spend. However, they will first make sure you are in business for real and they will do that before giving you a penny. It really takes work and patience. I have been preparing for two years and learning for over nine. My goal is to cut out seven years of the learning curve for you to the best of my knowledge and ability.

So, do your research on the topic. See if you can get a book on the subject from the library for free and always do your due diligence on the author or personality. What I discuss in this book is primarily from my personal life experiences. You will still have to do a lot of your own research to get where you need to be. My goal is just to get you going and motivate you to take ACTION!

What is poverty?

Poverty is hunger. Poverty is lack of shelter. Poverty is being sick and not being able to see a doctor. Poverty is not being able to go to your school of choice. Poverty is the result of not knowing how to read. Poverty is not having a job with bills and debt. Poverty is making $5.15 an hour in a $15.50 an hour world. Poverty is working because you have to not because you choose to.

Poverty has many faces changing from place to place and across time. Poverty can be described in many ways. Most often, poverty is a situation people really want to escape. I have never met anyone who said they desire to stay broke and in poverty. NEVER! IF YOU DON'T GET OUT OF THAT COMFORT ZONE OF BEING BROKE, YOU WILL FOREVER BE IN POVERTY! Poverty needs to become your past. You should use it to propel yourself into a better future.

Most people never change because they are so comfortable in the place that they are in and are AFRAID to make a change. That's right, I said you're scared. That is the only thing it can be. Nothing else can stop you from making the necessary changes. Everything else can be turned around. The knowledge is free in the libraries and the people are there to help you. Even if you are in a bad abusive relationship, cannot read, come from a single parent home or are homeless right now. You can do it! Just make up your mind that the buck stops here and you are going in a new direction.

It will take some discipline, time and commitment but you can surely get it done. Some of you feel that you are stuck at that job and cannot do anything else because you have a family to feed and need the benefits. I will never say quit your job. Keep that job for now. It will make life a little easier. When your business starts to make some good money, you will know when it is time to walk away from the job. So, until you have made enough money to walk away from your current job, stay there and STOP digging the debt hole that you are in.

I was there, stuck in my poverty comfort zone. The more money I got, the more money I spent. I bought the new cars and had other toys. This was all bad debt that I had to work to pay off. Here's the kicker: With all that debt, I did not gain anything. Now, I ask myself before I buy anything whether this will be good debt or bad debt. It does not make a whole lot of sense to go and finance $50k or $60k for something that drops in value as soon as you drive it off the lot or take it out of the store. As bad as I WANT, not NEED a brand new 760i BMW or MB S600. I cannot see myself buying it new using my personal money.

Now, I have no problem letting one of my businesses pay for it as transportation for the President. Buying it straight out from my personal money, it is not going to happen. Plus, the new feeling will be gone in six or seven months anyway. That is one of the perks of having a business. The luxury stuff can be a business expense. It is an old strategy used by Entrepreneurs everyday. You really do not need to be buying anything of high dollar value without having your finances in order either. This means make sure you have the proper amount of cash in the bank or accessible somewhere in case of rainy days. The years 2009, 2010 and most likely 2011, will prove that we all need to be a lot more frugal with our money.

I would spend my money on an airplane before I would spend it on a car any day. The plane can get me and my business associates to business deals to make the money for the car. Use of an airplane would be a business expense also. So if it is luxury, tie it into a business expense. In today's market place, if you are doing big business, airplanes become necessities more than luxury.

I have two kids in the house year round. In the summer, I can have up to five kids; three of my four girls and two boys. We used to go and eat every time I made some money. Guess how much that was costing me? We average about $40 to $60 every time we went to a restaurant. Multiply that by three times per month, we are looking at spending $120 to $180 per month just for eating out.

Now, guess how long that lasted after I ran the numbers? That is basically $200 per month we can now invest monthly for our kids. The invested money could give them the cash they need for college and/or their future businesses. Just like you trim the fat off of meat because it is not all good for your health, you have to trim the fat off your finances because it is not good for you and your family.

You have to change the way you think about and do things. If you keep doing the same thing, you will keep getting the same old result. You will be like the hamster on the wheel. You will be running in place exerting a lot of energy never making any real progress, just busy being busy. Your mind and body will feel the affects of you putting in the work.

However, you wake up the next day in the same old spot. Think about it if we don't have something else other than our jobs to look forward to everyday; we are no different than the rat on the wheel. We get up, go to work, come home, sit in front of the T. V., go to sleep, get up the next day and do it all over again. This is called being STUCK in the RAT RACE. You are definitely racing, but you will never finish IF you don't change your game plan. You will not even get out of the starting blocks.

Still to this day, I let myself day dream about how it would have been if I would have gone to college to play football instead of going into the Army. I see guys I know I could have played with and been pretty successful at it. Although, I really loved jumping out of airplanes and being in the 18th and 82nd airborne corps. My dream was to play professional football in the NFL for the Atlanta Falcons or Dallas Cowboys. Due to the lack of money at the time when I had to make a decision about college, I chose the military. I knew then, even with a full ride at school, I would still be struggling from day to day...and I had enough of that.

No disrespect to my parents and family. We had wonderful times growing up. It all changed when I realized that my parents and family where barely making it. Lights would get turned off, water was disconnected and food would be low. It is this that motivates me to do what I do today. We were on government assistance. We had to use food stamps to buy food. Notice I said HAD too. I remember people who used food stamps who really did not need them. Some folks have to use it and some don't.

If you have to get assistance, go ahead; just understand that this is because you do not have enough residual income. I would not depend on the government to assist me for long. You should not either. Use the benefits as a stepping stone and leave the program for someone else to use as a stepping stone. Don't abuse the system because you will mess it up for the next person who really needs it.

I know a lot of you have had to wear high water pants before. If you have not, they are the pants that you basically grow out of and your parents cannot or chooses not to buy anymore. I remember going to school on peanut butter sandwiches. Man, now that I am thinking about it, things were really tight for my mother back then. That is why when I sell enough of these books and my businesses are strong, she will never have to work again in her life. There is one thing great I can remember. That mother of mine could and still can cook! She could take some left overs and make a whole new meal and it would be great. My other mom, Velma is the same way. The cooking has always been great.

Anyway, I did not grow up with a silver spoon in my mouth. It was more like a plastic spoon but we got by and that is what mattered THEN! Now you cannot just get by. Times have changed and it costs more to live today and raise kids. Babysitting was not an issue when I was growing up. My mom could just drop me off to my Aunt's or Grandmother Annie Mae's home and that would be that.

Today, most moms do not live in the same city or state as their parents. So, that eliminates the option of dropping off the kids all together. Remember the past does not matter. You can still be financially successful. No person, handicap, reading disorder or economic situation can stop you. You can be broke as a joke right now and it still does not matter. Gaining knowledge is what is going to help you first get going. But, you say to me, Bobby, "I cannot even afford to buy a bag of chips, how can I go buy a $24 book"?

When I could not afford to buy a particular book, I went to the library, got a library card and checked the BOOKS out. I read THEM and returned them to the library. Sometimes I would turn them in late, because I needed to re-read them to really get the whole message. There is no excuse...just take ACTION...PERIOD. Action kills fear so take action!

Some books I mention will not always be at the library, so look on EBay, Barnes & Noble or Amazon.com. There are a lot of people who have used books that they will sell to you for just a few dollars. Eventually, you will find the money you need from tips in the books and get on track creating "Rivers of Wealth".

So again, no EXCUSES! Get a library card and start READING some books and listening to some audio tapes or CD's! I know you have or have access to a MP3 player. Download and listen to audio CD's on building wealth. When I am in my car, I play CD's that help me keep my mind focused on financial success and thinking big. Before I go to sleep, I try to read a chapter or two from a book that will educate me or give me some kind of nugget of gold or resource to help me grow. If you choose not to read or listen to motivational CD's, you will not be a wealthy or successful business person. You also will have little opportunities of being successful in life. All because you have not read and learned how to prepare your eye to see those opportunities.

There is a bible verse that backs that statement up, Hosea 4:6 – *"My people are destroyed for the lack of knowledge."* It did not say for the lack of money, stuff or people, but KNOWLEDGE. Get the knowledge and everything else will be gravy. It will all fall into place. The right knowledge will allow you to be very creative.

I blew through money especially when I was in the military. Never before have I had money to put in to my bank account every month like it was while I was in the Army. I would spend it before I ever got it and the stores and clubs didn't mind helping me do that either. That is what they were there for. They are in business to make money. It was all my fault and I accepted the blame for that and made a change. I look back now and say, man what if I would have known this or that back then? If I would have known what I know now, back then I would be closer to Billionaire status right now.

Look at the devastation of the hurricanes and how they left people without anything. I have been saying it from the beginning. The folks who had their financial house in order; meaning had the MONEY to get out of those areas...DID! Do not get me wrong here. I wept and still feel hurt when I see what those folks are going through. I wish I had a billion dollars to give right now to help them out. This is another great benefit of have massive wealth. You will be able to contribute to others at the drop of the dime.

Here is my point: After all is said and done, it comes down to MONEY. If you do not have money in this society, there are just certain things you will not be able to do. Unfortunately, health care and basic living expenses are key components that we have to have access too. People work to live and live to work, all the while never earning enough. The price of everything today is up and the pay check is still the same.

So, if there has never been a wake up call in your life to forget about the past and move to a secure financial future, whatever the vehicle, seeing the people who suffered through these hurricanes should be. That's why I am such an advocate for Direct Sales/Network Marketing. I believe it is the easiest way to start and grow a business (Rivers of Wealth) without someone holding a check over your head. It does not have to be your dream business, but just the first of your many "Rivers of Wealth". We will talk all about Direct Sales later in another chapter.

All the money mistakes you have made don't sweat them. Learn from them and keep moving. Who cares about what they did or what you did not have in the past. The question is what are you going to do about the situation right now? That is all that matters today. Start right now from zero with whatever you have even if it is one dollar. You have the potential and the opportunity to turn that one dollar into one million dollars. You can do it if you discipline yourself and be persistent.

My mom and dad were never rich nor did they teach me about becoming wealthy. I learned that from being very broke, destitute and in poverty. I did not know how to manage my personal credit. I learned that from being bankrupt, evicted, homeless and having my car repossessed. I learned how to become wealthy because I did not have anything. I was in debt up to my head and I did not like how it felt at all. I also had young children and a family that depended on me. That was more than enough incentive for me to get my act together. What is your Why? What will it take for you to get your act together?

Let's Get Started

I need you to read, read and read some more! Start at gaining knowledge. Do not go and try to start your business right now, YOU ARE NOT READY! Get the books I recommend and READ them a couple of times, then go to step two.

The only business I would recommend you going into while learning is Network Marketing. The initial investment is minimum and you get a mentor to help you along the way. We like to say you earn as you learn. Someone could come and give you $50,000 to start a business today but without the proper knowledge, you will most likely fail. You have to read everything you can. Ladies put down the romance novels. Guys put up the play station and the Wii's or whatever it is these days. Pick up the Wall Street Journal, USA Today, and your local newspaper. Read the business sections and listen to my radio show. You can visit the website anytime, www.norrsonmedia.com for show information.

You will also need to get a few mentors. These people will be willing to help you succeed simply because you want to become successful. It is very important that you get a mentor. That means you will have to start networking with successful Business Owners and Entrepreneurs in order to feel people out. Determine who you think would be a good mentor for you. I have multiple mentors. I try to keep a mentor for every aspect of what I do. I have a real estate business. I am mentored by someone who is SMARTER than me in Real Estate. Spiritually, I have a few mentors and in my general business practices I also have mentors.

I keep a mentor for each type of industry. Now you will not have as many mentors as I do. You might only have one or two businesses. Just make sure that you can trust the person and they are on the up and up. Take your time in finding a mentor. Do your "Due Diligence" on them. They will check you out to see if you're serious. The last thing a successful person will do is waste time with someone who is not serious about business. We pick up on B.S. quickly.

Until you find a mentor, just start networking with other business people in your area. Find and maybe join a local business networking group and get into the mix of things. There are plenty of groups out there to join. Look in the newspaper for upcoming events and meetings. There are women in business groups, men in business groups, groups for motivational speakers and referral groups. You name it and there is a group of people who get together on a regular basis, visit www.meetup.com and see what you can find. Once you get the feel for these groups, you will know how to pick a good local one yourself.

WARNING...DO NOT get involved in the "it's a business gathering" and the only business going on is drinking and mate chasing. Successful businesses are built by serious minded no-nonsense people, not party hoppers. So if you are still in that stage of your life, you are not broke enough and you are definitely not ready to build an Empire. In order to become very successful, you will have to change your habits. Believe it or not, success is really turning your poor habits into good habits and perfecting those habits on a daily basis. See you in the next chapter.

Norrson
Media Group

"Knowing is not enough; we must apply. Willing is not enough; we must do."

Johann von Goethe

Chapter 3

Change Habits, Stay Focused

"One habit at a time equals great success"

I was once asked by a young man I was mentoring, how he could get out of the financial and life ditch he was in and I simply replied, "Stop digging!" Really, it is as simple as that. Stop digging the hole and start filling that hole with knowledge. This will give you the power you need to pull yourself up and move forward to a positive financial future. I know you want change in your financial life which is the reason you are reading this book.

That's what this chapter is about. Making that change and improving the quality of your financial life. By reading this far, I know without a doubt that you will be successful in anything that you set your mind to do in life. You have stayed focused and that is a very great thing. I can not wait to see you at the top.

So okay, in order for you to improve your financial situation, you must first stop digging the hole that takes you deeper and deeper in debt. Leave the cash advance places alone. Stop taking pay advances from your place of employment and DO NOT open anymore credit card accounts. STOP IT, STOP IT, STOP IT! Believe me, I know this will hurt in the beginning but you will be very glad you stopped in the end. Either way you look at it, you are going to face a hard transition into this new way of life, but the storm does not last always. STOP GOING IN REVERSE, change gears and move forward!

I am going to give you some good news. This is not all your fault. Your upbringing and early financial atmosphere had a lot to do with your current situation. However, you are now responsible for "Stopping the bleeding" as they say in the Army. One of the first things we as soldiers were taught to do when we came upon an bleeding soldier was to stop the bleeding. After we stop the bleeding, then and only then could we assess the problem and put a plan into action to get that soldier medical attention.

You are no different. The only difference is that your wounds are debt wounds and not only are you wounded, but you have been locked into an invisible cage called "Financial Illiteracy". There is no need to worry anymore. I have found you and I will break the lock off the door of your cage and free you. We will gain financial freedom step by step together....Let's Go!

You were exposed to a certain group of habits growing up and this carried over into your adult life. Since you were not in the HABIT of seeking wealth and abundance, you never improved your financial knowledge or quality of life. That is why I stress to current and would-be parents to start teaching their kids great financial habits as soon as you can. This will help them a great deal in life.

There are tons of opportunities missed by those of us who did not have a strong foundation in Wealth building techniques. Just as we as a society stress educational and good grades, we must DEMAND financial literacy from our youth. Once again, it will make a huge difference in their quality of life. Hell, it will make a huge difference in YOUR quality of life! I have made sure my kids understand the difference between a profit and a loss, poverty and wealth. I taught them the difference between the subjects very early.

They also have a good understanding of the difference between wants and needs. There are a lot of THINGS we want but do not necessarily need.

Check this out, I was reading in the business section of a local paper a few days back about the sub-prime mortgage melt down. The article was talking about how the default percentage went up very high in the month of December 2007 and they speculated that this was because people had to make a choice between Santa and their mortgage. This was the same in December 2008. What do you think most people chose? Yep, they took Santa over the mortgage, BAD move, and BAD habit!

I know you did it, I did it before. Most people have chosen Santa over the mortgage. They knew if they would have done the right thing, there would have been no money left over for Christmas. We have got to stop living for now and start living for the future. Ask the question: Needs verses Wants? Christmas presents are wants not needs. Don't even get me started about the real reason of Christmas. We have got to get in the habit of taking care of our finances first and make our wants last. Who cares if you have a big screen T. V. or the current year car? Don't be a conformist. Stand out on your own. Do your own thing. Forget what people think. The fastest way to fail in life is to try to keep up with the Jones. They are broke too and it will not work.

Your habits determine your future and exactly how successful you will be. Therefore, if you do not like your current situation, just change your habits and you will see a dramatic change in your total quality of life. It is very, very important that you change your BAD habits into GREAT habits. More so when it comes to your finances, habits are essential. Take a minute to imagine yourself 10, 20 or 30 years from now. Do you want to be working because you have to or because you want too? There is a big difference between the two situations.

I remember reading an article that showed that ONLY 3 out of every 100 people in America would be able to actually enjoy retirement. These will be the 3 out of 100 people who have disciplined themselves as it relates to finances. They will be able to do what they want and go where they want at anytime. I really hope to change this number. I know that there are some folks who are not going to listen to one word I or any other wealth or life coach has to say. Some folks just have bad habits and refuse to work to change them. Those are the folks you need to stay as far away from as possible. I just hope that we can have more than 3 out of 100 people able to become financially secure and live their dreams with passion.

Are you setting yourself up for that type of lifestyle or are you living one day at a time? If you are living one day at a time, you are setting yourself up for financial destruction and a life of poverty. If you are going to work everyday, building the first part of your life, shouldn't you enjoy the second half? Change those habits and you will change your life for the better. This change should be an everyday practice, a new part of your lifestyle.

You can not take a pill and expect it to be all done. Life does not work like that. You cannot make millions overnight, as many schemers would lead you to believe. You were not born overnight. Remember success takes time. Understanding this will help you along the way and you'll enjoy the ride much more.

You are where you are today because of the habits you have adopted over time. When you get out of your car, do you lock your door and check to make sure your head lights are off? When you get in the house, do you put your keys in a certain part of your purse or pants? Is there a hook where you put your keys or coat so you can see them for the next trip out or do you just throw them on the nearest chair or counter and spend 15 minutes looking for them when it is time to go somewhere else? Now after spending 15 or 20 minutes looking around for those keys, you are late again and frustrated. Look how your day has started off. Whose fault is it? It is YOURS. This could have been prevented.

I know sometimes you just throw stuff down and keep it moving. You are that lady I see in the mornings putting on the makeup in the car at the stop light. That reminds me of something. I remember going to church one morning, oops...I lied. We had skipped Church and were going to the beach this particular Sunday. What? ...it was a hot sunny day! Anyway, we were at the light and a van pulled up next to our car. When I looked over at them, I first saw a man. I assume the man driving was the father. Then I saw two females, which were the mother and daughter. Do you know that both the mother and the daughter were putting on makeup at the light at the same time? My point is this is a habit mom is passing down to daughter, which says: it is okay to get up late, be unprepared and put your makeup on in the car.

I am going somewhere with this. Stay with me on this. Fast forward ten years, daughter is now 21 in the car putting on makeup because she still has a habit of running late. Distracted, she gets in a fender bender and it costs a couple of hundred dollars to fix her car. Now if she had changed that habit and gotten up maybe an hour or two before she needed to leave the house, the road would have had her full attention and maybe this accident would never have occurred. When we rush, we put ourselves in a bad position where accidents can happen. It all has to do with habits, do you get the point?

To this day, I still don't get up when I am really supposed to be up. I am awake but it is just so hard to come up from under those nice warm covers. This usually leads to me being late getting to where I need to be and I don't like that. So, to fix the problem, I committed to really focusing on changing that habit of not letting the covers go. My goal is to be up and about two hours before I ever have to leave my house. This will give me enough time to do whatever it is I need done.

If you're like me and you tend to run late a lot, try getting up two hours before you need to leave the house. Let's say you have to be at a meeting at 8:30am, try getting up at 6:30am. Now, you can move slowly through the house and let your brain take in the fact that you are actually up. You will have time to make some coffee or tea and eat a nice breakfast. It is very important to have a good breakfast. You can also read the business section of your morning paper and check your email. Always check your email in the morning, that way you can respond to important ones that day.

If you check your emails at night, sometimes you take that business to bed with you and you don't need that. Now you are ready to take a shower and get dressed to conquer the world. All this and you will be on time, unless a water main breaks or something like that. Bottom line, you have done your part and changed a habit which improves the quality of your life. That is success. You changed your habits and it affected your life in a positive way. It was positive because those adjustments or changes relaxed you and zapped out some stress. Now let's do that with your money issues and really make some changes!

Whatever habits are to you, they are your habits and they determine how smooth or how not so smooth your life is and will become. Changing your habits can have a direct effect on your current financial situation. Do you spend more time watching T.V. than reading books or listening to tapes that will help improve your financial situation? Do you network with others who have changed and/or are trying to change their financial situation for the better? Do you hang out with people who are content with where they are and are not lifting a finger to do anything different to better their financial future? You know who I am talking about, those "Oh...I got a good job" people. I have said it before and I will say it again, **THERE IS NO SUCH THING AS A GOOD JOB!** You do not build wealth with a job. You build wealth by owning a small business in the USA. Entrepreneurship is the way to build massive wealth.

Changing your habits will not be easy. It will take some time, discipline and persistence on your part. You will need to be and stay focused as much as possible. You should start with something small like putting your car keys in the same spot every time you put them down. If you like to get a few extra minutes of sleep in the mornings, start small by getting up 5 minutes early then increase it to 10 minutes.

Changing bad old habits was very hard for me. In writing this book, I put it down so many times. I did not really change my writing habits. I kind of just wrote when I was inspired. I would make excuses like "Oh, I will just do the book on CD...people don't really read anymore" or I would write on the weekends. I didn't stay focused and instead of the book and CD being ready for a December 2005 release, it did not come out until late 2009.

Here is a simple statement. If you would like to be a bum, hang out with bums and they will be happy to show you how. You can stand on the street corner everyday hoping that someone will hand you their pocket change and then head back to whatever shelter you have and do it all over again the next day. Think about it, even those folks on the highways and byways have a set of habits, often bad habits in my opinion, but they are habits.

Now, I do not know what brought those people to that point and I don't want to come off as insensitive. However, anyone on this planet can change their life if they only just change their habits. There is a group of people who are just kind of stuck in the life that they have because of extreme mental, physical or substance abuse issues. Even with drug addictions, some people have been known to fight back and turn their lives around.

On the other hand, if you would like to be wealthy, I mean really financially free and secure. You should begin to hang out with and network with people who are and who have done just that. These folks are like minded and they will be happy to show you how. This is essential in your new "Building a better life" plan. You have to have an ACTION PLAN!

This book is for those who are mentally and physically capable of changing their lives. For most people, it will be extremely HARD, but the pleasure is well worth the pain. The question you should ask yourself is: What am I willing to do today that will ensure that I will be able to do what I really want tomorrow and for the rest of my life?

Changing most habits takes some time and it will not happen over night. Some of your habits have been in place for so long that it will take a few months to change. At least you can identify them and begin the process of change. Only when you decide and begin to change your habits for the better, will your life: Financially, Spiritually, Physically and Mentally improve. Don't be offended, but a great part of why we are in the poor financial position that we are in is because of ignorance. We invest in everything but financial education.

That's right! Ignorance is what is keeping us from enjoying all of the great benefits that life has to offer. Why is it that only 10% of Americans enjoy complete financial freedom and 90% don't? They are no different from you. You have the same mental capacity....So what's the problem? The difference is that 10% works harder, longer and they are up before you every morning.

They invest daily into their knowledge bank, educating themselves about wealth building. They are also still up when you lay down at night to go to sleep. They read more and they put themselves in the networking groups that help them grow. They surround themselves with people that are smarter than they are. They are passionate about their dreams. They are also so stubborn that failing is seen as a learning experience and not the end. They don't quit, even when they feel like all is lost.

Now having said all of that, I have some great news for you. Most of you think that ignorance is something that cannot be overcome but it can. Ignorance is nothing more than a lack of knowledge in a certain subject or area. We are all ignorant in a few subjects and areas. What determines our success in life is adopting new learning HABITS that will turn our ignorance into knowledge. Then we take that knowledge and use it as power to obtain success, whether it is physical, mental, spiritual or financial.

Being an entrepreneur and CEO sometimes spoils you when times are good for your business. I can remember times at Jiacom where there were no real pressures and no real milestones. I was not focused on obtaining goals because money was flowing in and I slacked off. I had a false sense of security and I changed my normal business habits. Instead of getting out of bed a 5am and starting my day, my day would start around 9am or 10am. I would not get to the office until that afternoon. When I got to the office, I would call friends and talk on the phone about nothing all day and then leave my office. Can you imagine how much valuable time I wasted? In essence, it set me back and I had to work extra hard to grow the business later.

I was not returning calls from clients and vendors or even really planning for the next move my company could make to become more successful. As a result, the company suffered. I had to start all over re-planning and changing my habits back to the way they were before I had a little breathing room. My point, do not get too comfortable just because things seem to be going good. Always stay in growth mode and continue to prepare to reap other harvests. Your goal on this new journey should be to grow and preserve as much money as you can while maintaining a healthy lifestyle.

Depending on where you are at in life right now is what will set your level of focus and determine your habit changes. If you're fresh and brand new pursuing this better financial life, you have to wipe your board clear right now. You need to imagine what you want your new financial future to look like and set out to get there. I mean really picture what you would like your life to look like and write it down some where you can see it everyday. Write down what amount of money you want to have, not just the amount you need to survive. This is the amount you want to have in excess of the day to day living expenses. I have a certain amount of money that I MUST have at my disposal daily. If the money gets below the set amount, I will do what is necessary to get it back to my desired balance.

Consistently Persistence & Staying Focused

Now that you know you have to change your habits in order to change your life, we need to discuss how to keep it all going. Once you begin to change your habits and you start really exercising those changes on a daily basis. You are going to feel this great sense of accomplishment. Then, it is going to happen! You are going to think you have it in the bag and get comfortable and lose the consistency that you started out with. You get complacent and you think, "I know this stuff already...it is second nature to me now". This is a big mental mistake.

Think about it like this. If you decided to get yourself into shape...I mean get the six pack abs, cut your body fat, eat right and all that other good stuff. Do you think you should do it until you reach your goal and stop? I dare you to try it and see what happens. If you do not maintain those pass habits, you will gain more weight and have to work harder at getting back to where you were than before. The same principles apply with changing and maintaining great financial habits.

You will have to monitor your habits on a daily basis and after a good bit of time of practicing these techniques, it will become second nature for you to question yourself about what you are doing. For example, I use to drink a lot of sodas...this is great for the companies that make it but bad for me. So I decided to break that habit as it would be a healthy choice for me. Well, I would go without a soda for about a good week and then WHAMM! Out of no where, I am guzzling down a big soda with a burger and some fries.

I made the decision to stop drinking sodas and start eating healthy, but as soon as I let my **WANTS** take control of my **NEEDS** the problems started again. So here I go, I now have to start all over again. Don't get me wrong, I still will have a burger and a soda...or two but on certain days only. There has to be some kind of fun in your life. Just don't have bad life habits everyday. It is very easy to stop at a fast food spot but it takes discipline to eat at home or take your lunch to work or the office daily.

Listen, you are going to do it...I KNOW YOU ARE! This is why I am writing about it. Remember I told you about myself and this very book you are now reading. It should have been done in the year of 2005 but I got comfortable and was not consistent. I let life get in the way and my priorities changed. The book did not get done until late 2009. That is almost fours years past due. If I would have stayed consistent, I would have hit my first release date. Other life's cycles have happened since then, which made the book more valuable, but maintaining great habits is essential. What are some of the things in your life that you have started and have yet to finish? There is a saying, "Why put off for tomorrow, that which you can do today?"

You know you need to get that life insurance policy, make that will and start investing. What is holding you up? You know you need to have a household budget to track your finances. You know you need to start that small business to create that extra income. Again, what's holding you up?

When you start these things, you will need to be as consistent as possible. That is going to take persistence. This will be your specific, achievable goal. The easiest way to stay on track is to adopt new habits and get better at doing them everyday. Being consistent is nothing more than staying focused and disciplined. It is not about doing one giant thing. It is about achieving one small goal a few times per day, everyday.

CEO of Me, Myself & I

No one else will take care of you better than you. Get in the habit of creating and practicing healthy habits that will enrich your life. If you do not take care of you, you will not be able to create any real change in your life. You have to be in the habit of getting enough sleep, eating right, reading and working out. The atmosphere in your home needs to be relaxing and harmonious, married or not. The relationships you are in, be it friends and/or associates, should all be positive ones. If there is ANY negative in your life, GET RID OF IT FAST! That includes people, places, thoughts and things!

Make it a habit to take time for yourself to reflect and search for answers to issues and obstacles that present themselves each day. This type of time is very important. I call it meditation and it really works for me. The problem lies in being persistent about meditating consistently. The more organized and centered you are, the less chances you have of failing badly in the future. Notice I used the word badly because if you are not failing, you are not trying. Pitfalls are a part of the success process. The faster you learn and accept this, the faster you will build wealth.

So, you see everyone is a CEO in a way. You are the person responsible for shaping, growing and maintaining the business of your own life. Not to mention, if you have children, you are responsible for their lives up to a certain point. It is not our government's job to give you a comfortable lifestyle, it is your job. The government or your job should not determine when and where you retire, you do.

If you don't plan and build wealth, they will however tell you exactly what to do and there will be nothing you can do about. They will determine how much medical coverage you get, when you can take vacation and what you will do on a daily basis while at work. That is not really total freedom. When I hear someone talking about waiting until they get 60 or 65 to retire, I cringe. I am working on that retirement thing to be when I am 45 or 50. Although, I do not intend to really ever retire, I do have a goal of being independently wealthy by that time. That way if I decide to take three months off and live in Hawaii, I can. You have the option of doing the same thing, you can just live or you can live your dreams.

The system I intend to use to obtain that goal of total financial freedom is to continue changing my bad habits into what I view as great ones. I believe by repeating and mastering this practice everyday, I will obtain what I view as success in my life.

5 Great Habits

Start with these five great habits if your life is in the pits. Practice adopting these habits until you see some improvement and then add more great habits to your tool chest.

1. Keep a Positive Attitude

Everyday you live, there are going to be people and things that are designed to take you off path and change your focus. The people will be those who have a miserable life and want you to be in the boat with them. They find all the bad things about situations and never see the benefits of things. Remember what I said earlier. Get and keep negative people out of your life. I don't care who they are, if yo mama is negative...guess what, you can't talk to her a lot......yep, I said Yo Mama. **What?** I am from the south....we say MAMA☺! I do know what we label as proper English. **Relax!** The point is, negative people are like cancer, it will slowly KILL you, if you don't start to remove it from your system.

You will get frustrated, mad as hell and sometimes even want to quit. The new habits goal you should have for yourself can be to try and find the silver lining in the situation. When a problem arises, ask yourself this, say "SELF...what can we learn from this situation?" Nine times out of ten, SELF will answer you and you will see that the situation is not that bad. Self is nothing more than your sub-conscience mind providing you with the right answer. Example, just yesterday, I was worried about getting more exposure for my new radio show. I was trying to reach out to sponsors to get a partnership deal done. No one was calling me back as fast as I would have liked. Bills were due to media companies and the salesperson I hired was not returning my phone calls.

I picked up the phone to call a friend to get her to call a national radio personality who could help me get my show off to a great start. Within seconds of the phone call, she was telling me about a car accident that her husband had been in a few nights earlier. Because I know her husband, I immediately forgot about my issue and focused in on hers.

Her husband was still in the Intensive Care Unit (ICU) of a local area hospital and she did not know what was going to happen. That phone call made me check for a silver lining in my situation. I was simply waiting for a phone call from potential sponsors. They would soon call and I knew sponsorship dollars would come. Why should I be worried or complain, I thought to myself.

I could be in ICU. Someone in my family could be in an ICU of a hospital somewhere. The point is somebody always has it worse than you and would jump at the chance to switch places with you. If you are not hooked up to tubes and can talk, STOP COMPLAINING! Suck it up....whatever the situation is and move on. Rada and Brian know that my Prayers are with you, your family will heal from this accident and you both will go on to do what God has set in place for you to do.

2. Reading Books and Listening to Tapes

The easiest way to become wealthy, I mean super rich is to READ! I don't know why people, especially black people, do not want to do this. Educating yourself in a subject will lead to a more fulfilling and secure life. So if you say you want to be financially secure, why don't you pursue the goal of being financially secure? I will tell you why, it is called FEAR. For some odd reason, a lot of people are afraid of succeeding because they are afraid of failing. However, if they just accept that failing is a part of the process to success, it would be a no-brainer to pursue their dreams with passion.

Okay, here we go anyway.....if you want to succeed in life, you have to read. Remember that saying, "There is nothing new under the sun", well the same holds true in business.

Everything you want to do has most likely been done. So all you have to do is find a book on the industry. Get some materials on some businesses in the industry and get started.

3. Become a Copycat

Habit number 2 leads right into habit number 3: Become a copycat. What I mean in saying this is you do not have to reinvent the wheel of business and wealth building. Everything has been done. All you have to do is LEARN the systems and implement them into your life to reap the benefits. Add a little bit of your own flavor to the mix and VOILA, you have your own Brand!

When I started my Internet access business, I did not just create that out of the blue. I made a decision on how much money I needed to make, found an industry that I liked and then found someone who had already became successful at doing it. I mapped the process they used and added my own little twist for my new business.

The key is to create a new and better way to do the same thing. Look at the apparel company Under Armor. This company came out long after Nike and Adidas. They do the same thing but they do it differently which brings them all success.

4. Networking with Like Minds

This is easy also. Start networking with people who are headed where you are headed. It will make the journey a lot more fun. Entrepreneurs support and motivate other entrepreneurs. When you mention building a million dollar home in a group of success minded people, you will not get crazy looks or negative reactions. You will get support and encouragement.

The things you do not know will be discovered by networking with other business owners. Deals will come to you first. This is what we call being in the "Deal Flow". Being in the "Deal Flow" allows you to grow your business faster and better. So simply put, stay away from folks who ain't trying to do anything and hang around folks who are...period. YEP, I said AIN'T!

5. Choose a Plan & Follow Through

Opportunity in America is sitting at every corner. You can do anything you want to in this country. Your mission is to find that something that is going to give you the dollar amount you must have. Then, work it until it can not be worked anymore. One of the main reasons businesses fail is not because of the business, but because of the founder not following through.

You have to make it your goal to accomplish a lot of small tasks each day and grow your business inch by inch, not mile by mile. If you do this, you will achieve all that you set out to achieve. Stay focused, follow through and you will win.

Once again, I know that the option to become financially secure is available to you should you decide to take it. I pray that you will take it.

I look forward to seeing you at the top.

Norrson
Media Group

"Most people achieved their greatest success one step beyond what looked like their greatest failure."

Brian Tracy

Chapter 4

Employee No More

"Flip the Script, Become the Employer"

Why Rivers of Wealth?

Like Oprah's quote, don't ever put a ceiling on yourself. You can do anything in this world that you put your mind to. It does not matter if you have no education, a high school diploma or an MBA. The playing field is now open to everybody, so go get it! If you want Millions or Billions, go get it. If you want Trillions, go get it.

You can either be an employee with your financial future in your employers' hands or you can become an entrepreneur who has a contract with your employer. The goal should be to have other income sources coming in besides the monthly pay check from your place of employment. The only way to truly become wealthy is to have some type of full-time business or a part-time business on the side that is producing the income you need. This will allow you to invest in and take advantage of opportunities as they come along.

Like right now, the mortgage industry is catching hell. They are reaping what they have sewn. They gave all these folks mortgages they could not afford and now mortgage defaults are at an all time high. However, this means opportunities exist for those who are financially able to take advantage of them. Builders are leaving $30,000,

$50,000 and as much as $200,000 equity in homes just to sell them. Imagine being able to buy a property that has $70,000 equity in it that you can use to grow your business even more. Man, you could get your dream home and make money at the same time. It is June 2009 and people are closing deals like that as I type the letters on this page. Why not you?

Everyday I see people get up and go to work. They leave work and come home. Then get up and do the same thing all over again the next day. THIS IS INSANE! Yes, it is insane if you are doing this and want or need to increase your wealth especially if you have dreams, kids and/or a need for medical or dental coverage. Listen, I know that companies are not providing any kind of real dental coverage, so if nothing else you should have money to keep that grill fixed! For those of you who are not up on the slang, GRILL is another term used for teeth. You see, there is a need for extra cheddar or shingles (more slang for the word money) in everybody's pockets.☺

Like I said before, there are over 30 million people living in poverty in America alone. Over 40 million folks are without medical or dental benefits. Do I really have to give any more reasons why more people need to have "Rivers of Wealth"? It is required for your future and the future of the generations that shall follow you. Don't try to tell me this is not true. I hear you at work after a nice weekend wishing it would never end. I see you getting up in the morning mad because you have to get out of that nice warm bed and go to work in that very cool weather. I see you in traffic complaining because you just got cut off. Only if you had enough money in your bank account, you would not be out on the road this early in the morning. I SEE and HEAR you, help is here!

Just one job with one income just won't cut it in this world today. Most of you have kids or a family and did I say, one job with one income will not cut it....oh....okay. Businesses are cutting back everyday now. They are laying people off by the tens of thousands and inflation is going up everyday. Have you seen the gas prices or are you living over in Lah-Lah land like nothing is wrong? Employers are making sure they cover themselves by cutting cost. You are a part of that cut, believe it or not. Job security is a thing of the past. Job security was strong in the industrial age; but we are now in the information age. Things move much faster now and the makeup of our society is very different.

The only security you can get today is the security you create for yourself and your family! THERE IS NO SUCH THING AS A GOOD JOB! If you believe that there is such a thing, you are in for a world of hurt. Unfortunately, because of the type of world we live in your good job will be handed to a younger person who is willing to work for less.....and work 7 days a week without complaining. Another possible outcome is your job will be taken over by a computer or machine. Machines can work 24-7-365! They do not need a lunch break, sick days and they don't complain or sue for equal rights...they just work.

What do you think the self check-out lane in the grocery stores, post offices and airports are there for? When I fly now, I don't even go to the airline check in counter unless I am checking a bag. I print my ticket at home on my own computer. That is someone's GOOD job gone just like that. If the company can get a machine to do what you do, you better watch out. Like I said, they don't talk back, request benefits, file labor charges, need lunch breaks and they can work 24-7-365. The trick is to become the person who services and fixes the machines when they need it. As sure is the sky is blue, some idiot will break or jam the machine and then the company has to call you, the technician who owns his/her business.

Another benefit to having Rivers of Wealth is that you will always have Disposable Income. For you all who do not know what Disposable Income is, it is money that is free for you to use on whatever comes up and/or money you CAN afford to lose. Imagine that; being in a financial position to be able to say, "Oh that $10,000 I lost on that last small investment deal was disposable income. It did not hurt my financial standing at all".

When you have disposable income, you have a greater sense of peace. Money will not bring this peace. You should have that peace before you become financially secure. Having wealth will add to the peace and satisfaction you already have knowing you can do anything in this world. You can get on an airplane and just go whenever you like, wherever you like.

You should have Rivers of Wealth so you can pass something to the generations that follow you. It is said that the Kennedy family had a hundred year financial plan. Why not you? You can commit to $25 per month for the next hundred years. This will setup your great, great, great grandchildren. How good is that for a head start in life? I will be at peace knowing my kids and theirs will not have to go through what I went through.

Here is a tip. Since we are living in the technology age; record video DVDs explaining to the generations that follow you on how important financial literacy is to a healthy life. Tell them your story and how you want much more for them. Give them resources like books and wealth building DVDs. This way they cannot say no one ever told them.

This I believe will be the greatest gift you could ever give them. This is also something they can pass on. It is history. You should record as much of it as possible.

Poverty is not something you leave to your family. If you are a living, breathing, semi-healthy human being and you are doing nothing to give your kids the upper hand in the future, you are a sorry excuse for a person! Yep, I said it. If you are not doing all you can to make sure your daughter doesn't have to strip to pay the bills and feed her kids or your son doesn't have to steal, or sell drugs to live, you are a sorry....#(%&@(!!#)&%^@.

Life is already tough enough. Even if you have to work a full and part time job to get to where you need to be, DO IT! I worked for the US Postal Service and for an airline part-time at the same time just to get ahead. It was not that I did not make enough to live off at the post office, I did. The problem was I did not have much left over to use for Wealth building. So I ran my business and worked part-time for a few months to get myself ahead. This was much better than sitting up until 1am and 2am worrying about stretching dollars, robbing Peter and Paul to eat. Yep, I said robbing Peter and Paul. I had to rob them both to pay the bills! When you are broke, it will stress you out. You will not be able to sleep well and you experience other health related issues.

If ants are smart enough to gather a harvest in the summer, surely you can discipline yourself to make sure your kids have financial training to succeed in life. There is no excuse and it does not matter where you are in life right now. If you choose to create a better financial outcome for yourself and your family, you can!

I speak from real life experience. I know exactly how it feels not to have enough money to put gas in the car, feed the family and have to borrow a few dollars everyday from close friends. I made some bad financial decisions. I was not properly prepared and educated in the money area. I changed that and became financially secure. This will lead to me someday becoming a Billionaire. Now most of you might not be looking to make millions or billions, but at least you can put forth an effort to create a couple hundred thousand to get yourself in the proper position for financial success.

Life is not meant to be lived in poverty, yet at the time of the writing of this book, over 30 million people in the US alone are living in poverty and over 40 million people do not have health or dental insurance. Now that we are in this recession, those numbers are higher. Remember, recession means OPPORTUNITY for those who are in position.

That means right now as you read this book, a child's mouth and head is hurting because they can not go to get dental care for their teeth. There is someone in serious pain that does not have the money to go to urgent care. I keep repeating it because this is crazy and someone has to pay for it. So remember, keep your job for now for the benefits and begin increasing your net worth. Some of the possible rivers I talk about later can help you do that. There are plenty of rivers you can choose from. The key is just to pick at least three and get started today! Imagine it, get the knowledge and build the business!

If you only create an extra $300 per month, that's a start. You could invest half of that and become a millionaire in 20 years. Stop thinking about fast money and trying to get instant gratification. There is no pill to take to become wealthy. Wealth building takes time. It will eventually take on a snowball effect, but you have to get started. What you will see in the process as you save and grow your money is that there are plenty of other easy ways to create passive and/or residual income. You will get the wealth building bug and you will not stop at $300 per month. You will have the eye for opportunity which will help increase your net worth.

If you follow the basic principles of this book, inflation, neither your business nor your employer will affect your life or lifestyle financially with the ups and downs that WILL come. I suggest you get your hands on every book that speaks on wealth building and changing your life for the better. Listen to and read these books until you know the content like the back of your hand. This will condition your mind to see opportunities at every turn. Do this and I truly believe that your whole life will change for the better.

You should become Wiser, Healthier and Richer! Money is not the root of evil, the love of money is the root of all evil. I would even go as far as to say that the "Lack of Money" is the root of all evil. Show me poverty and I will show you crime. Let's get it right. Most broke people are not trying to do anything based on ethics. They are trying to figure out where the next meal is coming from. If that means committing a crime against you, then that is what it is going to be, real talk.

Pink Slip Protection Plan (PSPP)

The PSPP or pink slip protection plan is a backup plan in case your current or future employer or income (for self-employed) just happens to want to lay you off, move operations overseas, fire you (it is called downsizing now or becoming lean) or simply closes the business.

The PSPP is a plan that you have in place to manage the money you saved to live on until a new opportunity comes along. It is what you use to start that business or fund that college tuition for the kids. It is what allows you to keep peace of mind when everybody else around you is stressing out. You need this plan because most of you WILL get laid off, be fired or just become the victim of a business closing. You will need it because jobs don't come as quickly as they used to. Also, most of your new employers will not be willing to pay you what you were earning at your old position. Especially now, in 2009, there is a huge group of college grads who are eager to work and they WILL work for less. Work and life balance is more important to them than working 60 hours per week to keep up with the Jones's.

So remember, there will always be someone waiting in the ranks who will work for much less than you are earning. You are getting older and/or are already older, need I say more? The longer you stay with a company, the more they will have to pay you. The person that has been with a firm for 10 or 20 years will cost a company more than someone who has been there for only 3 years. Who do you think will get cut first? You should have a PSPP so that money is being earned while you have a steady income. This way you go to work happy instead of mad. The boss cutting hours will not bother you like it would someone who needs the hours. As a matter of fact, you will welcome less hours so you can go get some real business done or travel more.

Quiz Time! If you were to lose your current income, for whatever reason, how long could you survive off of what you have in the bank or in other assessable assets? Would it be 3 months, 6 months, 12 months, 24 months or 36 months?

Based on your answers, here is my assessment of you and what I recommend you do:

1 to 2 months: You are in real trouble. I have been there and you should finish this book and jump straight into SAVE MODE. Cut back on all extra spending now! Well, leave a pizza night and maybe...just maybe a beach trip one Sunday per month in the mix. If you are not close to a beach like me, an amusement park will do; but only for the day and don't spend a penny more than the budget calls for you to spend. I don't want to take the fun out of your life, but really how much more fun is it going to get if you don't get in control of your finances. Life is not fun if you are broke and stressed out all the time. If you only have one to two months stashed away, it is time for some real sacrificing.

Look at it this way, once you get your financial house in order, you can build from there. You can have more fun nights and longer vacations. For now, let's look at the current money coming in and see how much is going out. Then cut the unnecessary stuff ASAP, because this is what is killing you! Some well known authors would say that you do not need a budget, but I strongly disagree. Major corporations have financial statements and forecasts, why wouldn't you? They track what's coming in and going out. You should also treat your personal financial world the same way. You are responsible for the BUSINESS of your own life!

Let's talk about some of the unnecessary stuff right now. Cable T. V., this could be $30 to $100 dollars you can start saving per month. You don't need the T. V. right now anyway because you are supposed to be READING and listening to CDs on wealth building and big thinking! I know what you are thinking; Bobby, $100 is not a lot of money. Well my friend, I am here to enlighten you about what $100 can do. You can invest that $100 into a SAFE balanced mutual for 10, 15 or 20 years and have a hell of a lot more than if you were to leave it in the bank. That is a long time you say. Well remember I said it is time for sacrifice. If you do not sacrifice luxuries now, you will be doomed. You will find yourself working the rest of your life...most likely depending on someone else to take care of you. You tell me, what makes more sense, giving $100 to the cable company every month with ZERO return or putting it in a balanced mutual fund that can return hundreds of thousands of dollars? I have satellite TV, but my business covers that expense. You are not there yet, so it has to go!

There is a lady I used to work with. After 20 years on the job she was ready to retire. Well about 60 days out from her actually leaving the work place, I asked her in a round about way how she was planning on surviving in this tough economy. I know she was not getting much from retirement because companies don't pay that much for 20 years anymore. This lady who was in her early fifties told me that she would collect about $700 per month from retirement from our employer. She added that she and her husband had been investing their money for the last 20 to 30 years and were well prepared to enjoy their retirement.

After talking with her some more, I gathered that she invested about $300 to $500 per month for retirement. That meant that at 10 years gaining about 10% annual return they had about $103,000 in the bank. At 20 years, it would be about $380,000, and at 30 years they would have over $1.1 Million dollars in the bank for retirement. If you invest that $100, at 20 years, you would have about $75,000 in the bank. Wouldn't you rather have that verses nothing. At least with that money you can flip houses or buy tax liens and keep making money. The more you SAFELY invest the better your life will be.

If that means staying at your job for another 10 years to ensure you have millions of dollars in the bank, it is well worth the effort. Think of how empowering that would be to know that you are counting down to the day when you will not have to clock in anymore and have millions to show for it? How many people can say they will have $1 million dollars in 10 or 15 years? Look at the chart below and determine where you want to be in the future and put action plans in place to get there.

Making plans and taking action is a must. You have to determine what you want your lifestyle to be like. Then set the plan into action and keep it at that level even when you have millions of dollars in the bank. You will still be able to do everything you want. You will just have peace while doing it. You can still take vacations. Your mindset will be different because you are building the business of your new life and your new future. You can go to work smiling because you are on the road to real financial success.

The reason I talk about having the right mindset, is because most people do not succeed for that very reason. The way you think in life will carry you very far. You can have $5 million and lose it all because your mindset is wrong. The wrong mindset will allow you to bring the wrong types of people into your life. These people who usually have the wrong mindset will bleed your wallet dry and then leave you to hang out there. These are the folks you DO NOT want around you or your family...PERIOD!

Look at the hypothetical chart below, determine first how much money you want to have and take action to get it.

Your New Millionaire Success Chart

Assuming you are earning 10% on your investment.

By Investing	Wealth Created in 10 Years	Wealth Created in 20 Years	Wealth Created in 30 Years
$100	20,000	76,000	226,000
$200	41,000	152,000	452,000
$300	61,000	228,000	678,000
$400	82,000	304,000	904,000
$500	102,000	380,000	1,139,000
$600	123,000	456,000	1,356,000
$700	143,000	532,000	1,582,000
$800	164,000	607,000	1,808,000
$900	188,000	683,000	2,034,000
$1,000	203,000	759,000	2,260,000

You can accomplish this by cutting the small things out of your life. I mentioned the cable, cell phone bills, smoking and eating out all the time. There are people who invest their money every month. These are people who are earning more than 10% return on their money. The above chart is really doable if you really want it. So a new small business that is bringing in $500 to $3,000 per month could make you a millionaire. Your age and financial resources will determine what you should save. Someone who is 20 years old can get by with just $100 per month and be good for thirty years. However, someone who is 35 years old will need to invest a little more. If you are 35, maybe $250 per month for 20 years will be a good starting point.

VALUABLE TIP: Educate yourself on "Indexed Life Insurance". When my financial advisor told me about this financial tool, I almost cried. You really should look into this tool. My youngest son will not have to worry about money. I am taking the necessary steps to set him up now. It is not hard to do if you are willing to set your priorities and change your habits.

I know I struck a cord with a lot of you when I listed smoking as one of the things you can cut to save money. It is true. You know it just as well as I do. I know smoking is additive and quitting is one of the hardest things to do, but by changing this habit...it could make you wealthy and extend your life. In no way am I pointing the finger because people could say to me that liquor will kill me or beer will keep me from having that six pack stomach I am searching for everyday. The point is to change those habits as best you can, then invest that money so you can have a stress free financial life.

3 to 6 months: You are not in a lot of trouble but start or continue reading now! You should begin to seriously build from this good starting point. Remember, all it takes is an accident or loss of your job to start eating away at the money. So you really need to turn that cushion into something larger. Do not create any extra expenses for your household and stick to your budget. You might want to give yourself a raise by increasing your deductions and investing that money instead of giving it to the IRS to hold for you. So many people miss this huge money making opportunity or they manage it wrong. Increase the deductions, use the money to make some money and then pay the taxes that are due at the end of the year. Tax Liens might be somewhere you want to start looking. I would also look at Foreclosures. If you can buy and hold for awhile, you should reap huge rewards. Go to www.realtalkinvesting.com. Get Drew Solomon's CD and get started.

12 to 24 months: You are either very smart or have gotten a hands up. Do not take this position for granted. A serious illness could wipe that money out in a heartbeat. I have read stories of people having $300,000 plus in the bank and then came cancer. This one disease wiped them out clean and put them in a position they thought they never had to worry about. Keep building and never stop. If you don't need it, maybe you can help someone who does. Remember, it is always better to have money and not need it, than to need money and not have it.

If you are not dabbling in some small business, start one and enjoy it while you grow your finances even more. I am proud of you. Do not take any huge risks and only use some of that money if you really have to. Remember, hard times come and go. Those who have stored up in the good times will be at peace in the hard times.

36 months +: Great job, keep building the nest egg. If you have not yet started your dream business, you should consider starting it soon. You have enough money to take a chance or two. Start with something that you know has a good chance of working. Real Estate is always a good bet. Always buy low, sell high and duplicate the process. Even if you only make $10,000 per deal, you are still coming out on top. Try to do 5 deals a year and you will be adding $50,000 plus to your bank account and life should be just fine. Still read everything that can help you grow your financial knowledge bank. Don't get comfortable on me. Life can deliver you a blow too....stay up on your game.

Now, if you don't even have a week of pay set aside and I know that feeling, here is how to get it! First read every book that I have listed and every book they suggest. When you start reading, you will begin to apply the principles and thereby, you have begun. Second, start saving money and the other books you read will also tell you this. Try getting $50 saved in your bank account, then $100, $200 and on up until you get at least $1,000 in a savings account that is earning money that you do not touch! Remember, you can begin to save money by going to the library to check these books and CDs out. If they don't have them, they will order them. Every Entrepreneur should have a library card!

Not having one week of pay means you might need to take a part-time job or join a company with a direct selling/network marketing business model. The reason I say this is because a part-time job does not cost anything and are usually pretty flexible. The network marketing will cost you, but the potential return is great. The goal is to get some money in the bank for emergencies, not trips to the beach or Friday night dinners and movies! I don't care whose birthday party it is, you can't go. You won't have any fun anyway. Your lack of funds will be on your mind. Get them a card and keep it moving! You can party next year!

Let's assume you have done the work and now you have $500 to $1,000 in the bank. It is time to look at the credit you have a little closer and see what needs to be done to clean it up. You can now get one free credit report per year from each of the three credit bureaus. There is no excuse why you would not know where you stand with your credit. Just go to **www.annualcreditreport.com**. This will not give you the credit score. You can buy that for about $6 to $15 later. DO NOT allow any mortgage companies, banks, auto dealers to pull your credit. NOBODY pulls your credit but YOU. You should not be trying to finance anything right now anyway! When others pull your credit, it takes your score lower.

VERY IMPORTANT: This is a must because everything is or will soon be granted based on your credit score and history. Read any and all books on understanding and building your credit. As a matter of fact, there will be a new credit rating system soon. You need to fully understand how it works. Most businesses now use a credit check to determine if you will pay or not...that is the bottom line. They can deny you products or services you need for your business based on information in your credit report.

Companies are trying to figure out if they should trust you. Insurance companies say it is to offer you the best rate. However, the worse off your credit, the more money they can ask for. I really do not think they should be able to raise the rates the way they can, but I did not setup the system. Hospitals have their own credit rating system and they say they will not turn anyone away. We will have to wait and see about that. You already know to get a car and a home, your credit is going to be checked. Before the mortgage meltdown, it was very easy to get into a new home. Now you have to have your ducks in a row because companies are taking fewer chances on home buyers with shady or flawed credit reports. A 600 credit score used to get you into a home fast, now you need a 700 or 750 just to be taken seriously. This is why I am stressing the fact that you need to know what is in your report and how it affects you.

I can't wait to see the day when consumers start checking the credit of some of these major corporations. Then, we will have some real fun. Imagine a corporation trying to get your business and you ask for a copy of their Dun & Bradstreet report. They would probably fall on their face. Dun & Bradstreet handles business credit reporting for those of you who did not know. You can take a look at most businesses' credit just like they look at yours.

Try it one day and watch the looks on their face. Go to a car dealership and look around. Surely a salesperson is going to try and sell you a car that day on the lot. That is what they are trained to do. Don't buy anything and inform the sales person that you see something you like, but will have to check his company's credit history and complaint database before you buy. Ask the sales rep if he or she could provide you with that data and watch the look on their face. ☺

Okay back to your credit. There are a lot of other companies who gather data about you and I. They sell it to businesses so that they can make decisions on whether they will work with you or not. So watch who you are giving your information to and don't be afraid to ask them why they need it. Remember, the system we live and work in is built around credit. It will not however stop you from buying a house or a car. You don't even have to worry about it getting yourself a job, if you're an Entrepreneur.

Even for employment these days, they can check your credit, so watch out. I know you thought that after you got out of high school and college, there would be no more report cards. The credit score is the adult life report card. I got all failing grades on mine. This is why I am writing this book to help you and the generations that follow you. I was not educated on the credit system and how it worked. It cost me big time. You have to understand it and keep your credit good. Once you understand how the credit system works, it will not be hard to manage it. Get a copy of my other book, "Credit, Money, Power".

Now you have some money in the bank and extra money is still coming in. You know where you stand with your credit. You are ready to start looking for opportunities. There is no better place for a beginner to look than into Real Estate.

With a decent credit score and sometimes no money, you could make as much as $10,000 on one deal. I did exactly that with only $100 down on my first investment property.

Imagine this: You are making $45,000 a year at your job or in your business. You followed the principles in this book and all the books and materials you have listened to and read. By doing this, you got a part-time job to put up an extra $1,000 in your bank account. By the way, after you save that $1,000; you then get a CD and borrowed against it and started paying it back on time every month which in turn helps your credit score.

Okay, you find a few Real Estate deals that make you $90,000. If you lost your job or current income, there is 24 months of PSPP right there. It is really not that hard to do if you are serious. I only look for deals with at least $5,000 plus in them. Once you get an understanding of how it all works, you should too. Do not be deceived, you could do this while working a full time job!

Like I said on my first investment property deal, I put $100 up as earnest money and closed the deal. I found the deal in the local newspaper and met with one of the owners that same day. Being a real estate appraiser, I did my research and saw that the owners were selling the property for much less than it was worth. This made me think, I then started to ask the hard questions like: "Why are you selling a Gem at such a Price"? I thought he would tell me the roof needed to be replaced or that it had termites or a bad water leak…something that had to do with the physical structure of the house.

The owner I met with told me that he and his partner had decided to part ways and they were selling everything that they had invested in together. This made me happy and we made the deal happen. The property had about $13,000 equity in it when I closed the deal. Two years later the property had about $25,000 of equity in it. I'd say that was a real good deal for a first timer.

However, I did learn a few valuable lessons on this deal. You should take note of them if you ever plan to jump into real estate investing. If the Mortgage Company or bank says there are no closing costs, make sure that they do not roll it into the back of your loan. Make sure you get everything in writing before you sign any documents and take your time doing the deal. The only people who want to rush are the people getting money when you close. DON"T allow yourself to be pressured into signing anything, carefully read all documents! The deal is not going anywhere.

Here are a few key things to check when buying a piece of property. Check the roof, the Heating & AC, check for termites and water damage. If the house is really old, like 50's, 60's, 70's, and the 80's, the plumbing and electrical might cost some money so deduct that off of the asking price with your counter offer. The only problems that came with my deal were that I really did pay closing costs and the A/C went out. It cost me about $3,000 to fix.

I lost about $7,000 total, but I still made a nice profit from doing the deal. I also did not pay any real attention to the cost of the homeowners' dues and the covenant of the homeowners' association for the property. VALUABLE lesson learned. In all your real estate deals, avoid high homeowners' dues. Make sure that the homeowners' covenant does not allow them to foreclose on your property. If it does, DO NOT purchase that property!

I went from this 1,300 square feet property to a 2,300 square feet property with only $1,200 down. It was owner financed and with my sale price, I had about $25,000 equity in the property. The economy was getting bad at the time of the deal but I have no problem waiting. Since the economy is so bad right now, I am looking for land to build my dream home on. I am sure I can get a piece of prime land at a rock bottom price. You can too!

Sometimes unfortunate things push you into fortunate situations. It is all about how you look at the situation and what you learn from that which you are getting into. The man that THINKETH right... WINS! When you get settled with this process, you will begin to see opportunities a mile away. Making money and securing your financial future will be just another habit. This will be the habit that makes you an Employee NoMore and that will be GREAT!

Chapter 5

As a Man Thinketh

"Think Big, Win Big – Think Small, Get Small"

The Mind of an Entrepreneur

Do you have the mind of an entrepreneur? Do you desire to have the mind of an entrepreneur? What are you willing to sacrifice to gain the mind of an entrepreneur? You are what you think you are. The potential in you is limitless. Limitless value is in your mind. Your mind is the single most important tool you have. You can use your mind to either become extremely poor or extremely successful.

Regardless of what it is you are trying to accomplish, it all begins in the mind. There is a quote by Albert Einstein that says "Imagination is more important than knowledge". Now I know some of you are already saying, "No-Way". Yes WAY! Think about it. You first have to imagine a thing, before the THING can become a reality. Imagination happens in the mind. Then and only then do you go out and get the technical education to fulfill your dreams and destiny.

God speaks to us in our dreams with visions. We then determine whether or not we will pursue those visions. You know what visions I am talking about, not a vision of anything that is not of God. Those visions of the things you desire and ask for in Prayer.

When you are just sitting around or driving in your car, your mind wonders. It could be that you want a new car, so you imagine yourself driving that new car, even though the car you are driving is a broke down lemon. However, since you have imagined it, you can get it. This is something I learned from a multi-millionaire and business associate named James "Monte" Montague. Try it. It is the art of seeing yourself having that which you desire and it is very powerful.

Imagine yourself already in the possession of that dream car and then trace your steps backward. This will give you all the necessary steps you need to take to actually get the car. All you have to do is put together a plan and add action to it. You now have the ACTION PLAN. The goal is to pursue it relentlessly.

So dream big dreams and set your standards high. That will be the type of lifestyle you will have. Try to focus more on the outcome of a situation and less on the situation itself. Worrying about a problem does not solve the problem but searching for solutions to the problem does. Control your mind and it will take you to places beyond your wildest dreams. Controlling your mind will also lead to you controlling your body, your spirit and your money. Your mind will show you how to bring massive amounts of wealth into your life.

What is poverty?

Poverty is being really sick and not being able to see a doctor. Poverty is hunger, lack of shelter and/or being homeless. Poverty is not being able to go to school and not knowing how to completely read. If you live in the great United States, poverty is making less than $20K per year.

Poverty is being forced to scramble to get bills paid every month. Poverty is not having a decent job. It is the fear of what your future holds if you stay on the same path. Are you in POVERTY? Don't worry. If you really desire a better life, you are on the right path by reading this book and/or listening to my CD. I will help you turn your situation around with tips and nuggets of GOLD.

Above, I mentioned just a few of the many faces of Poverty. It changes from place to place and can be described in many more ways. I seriously believe that poverty is a situation that most people around the world painstakingly want to escape. Really, who wants to live in lack? Nothing good comes out of lack. All you get is crime and corruption when there is a great deal of lack. They even have T.V. shows now showing how people live when they are in poverty. Most of them would like to be out of that very horrible situation. The question is, how can they change their life and will they stick with their new action plan?

I believe that it all comes down to the last straw point with any person. That is, the point when they say to themselves that enough is enough. They don't want to be broke anymore and they are going to do something about it. Those that go forward with an action plan will become successful and those who just talk about it will stay in poverty. There is a saying, "Don't Talk About It, Be about It", which basically means stop running your mouth and show me something. Action is always better than talk any day.

Man, I have worked with so many people who said they wanted to change their financial lives. They really made me believe that they were prime candidates for success. However, once an action plan was in place, these folks would start and never follow through. I would put action plans together for them and show them exactly how to get a good jump on changing their lives. They would last for about three weeks and then just fade back into their normal routine. That is why 90% of Americans work everyday of their lives and only 10% of Americans are independently wealthy. Meaning, as it pertains to money they can do whatever, whenever and for as long as they want because money is not an issue. Do you want that lifestyle?

Now what is the big difference between you and them? You're Right...NOTHING, but they wanted it more and worked at attaining it everyday. They did not let life put them back into the same routine. They took ACTION, changed those habits, as we talked about in the last chapter and they STUCK TO IT! Most people don't pursue financial freedom because of FEAR. They are scared to fail. Not really understanding that failure is just a small part of the process of obtaining real wealth. These people do not want to change badly enough. Their thought process is still warped. How they feel about money and a new life is misguided and twisted.

WARNING: For those who do not get their act together, you will be experiencing extreme poverty here really soon. It is now the summer of 2009. In the upcoming years, there will be the haves and have nots. It is as simple as that! The middle class is going to be a thing of the past. These folks look and act like they have it all together but they are just a few checks away from being broke also. Most of them are trying to keep up with the Jones and the Jones are broke!

Take the average middle class family. Dad has a job making $90k per year and mom is a school teacher doing what she loves. They have two nice current year cars and take vacations on the regular. They have the perfect little family with two kids. They have a teenage girl and a young boy. They even have two dogs and a nice big fish tank in the basement of their $250k house with the big backyard.

These folks believe they have finally arrived. Life can only get better from here. They have not invested any money and the savings is limited, they might have $21,000 in the bank. Fast forward a few months and Dad's company is being acquired by a bigger company and now the job Dad had is in jeopardy because the new company has someone in the same position that dad currently holds. Only the person in the same position is 20 years younger and is being paid half of what the Dad is used to getting annually.

Now if you and I are taking over a company, who are we taking into that new company, our team or their team? Do we keep the person that makes more and is about to retire or the younger person with 20 years in front of him, who is working for less? Most likely we take our team and the younger person because we know these people and we think we can get more for less with them.

So, yep...you guessed it. Dad loses his job and now that $90K plus annual income is now $20K. Since, the family did not save or create any additional income it will not be long before financial stress creeps in the door. This will lead to confusion and all sorts of issues you would never think this couple would have. Whose fault is it? What was their thought process and why didn't they plan for this? It was their fault because of how they thought about life and money. The way you think about and see money will determine your place in life. You should understand money just like you understand anything else that is important to you.

You might think, oh...Bobby that is a stretch. There is no way someone with that type of money is going to make that kind of mistake. Those people plan and plan. They are smart which is why they have what they have in the first place. If you don't believe that this is happening all across the US, you need to pick up a newspaper. Almost, everyday you can read about some company laying folks off in droves. I mean laying people off by the thousands. A lot of these folks did not even expect or plan for it. It just happened. Your mind has to be strategically focused to see the writing on the wall. At that point, you can plan for any major changes in your finances.

In 2009 and beyond, I believe the key is for us to live a more frugal lifestyle. Even the wealthy rent some of their luxury goods. DON'T believe all the hype you see. When you see me in an exotic car, you can bet your bottom dollar, it is leased or rented and one of my companies is paying for it. That is one of the beauties of being in business.

Now back to my point and the above fictitious family. I believe that there is no such thing as a good job. Here is my reason for making that statement. If the corporation has to tighten its financial belts, the employee is always at the top of the list to get cut. Think about it for a minute. If a company is paying you $80K, $90K or $100K per year, how easy is it today to go and find someone who is willing to do that same job for $40K per year? Very easy and companies know this. It is happening everyday and you better plan for it or you will be caught in the cross fire.

Now, imagine if that same couple I spoke about was smart and had read the books you and I know about and read. Let's say, they saved money and lived on less than they were earning. This is called living below your means. There is nothing wrong with that. You can have a pretty decent life this way, if you properly plan. Richard B. Moore, the President & COO of my media company (Norrson Media Group) has this down to a science. Let's say, the family was making $90K per year. They keep their lifestyle at $60K per year. They now have $30K per year to invest and create other passive income. They decide to save $15K per year in a safe investment vehicle and use the other $15K for more risky investments.

The New Mindset

They are thinking differently now, so stay with me. One "River of Wealth" I will talk about later is tax liens and I am going to use this as an example now. Okay, they have $15K to use to put into something that could earn them some extra cash. Buying tax liens is basically when a property owner does not pay the taxes on their property. The Government can take control of the property and sell the property at an auction for a dirt cheap price to recover what they are owed in back taxes. An individual can pay those taxes on that property to the tax office and/or the Government agency and in a few months to a year own that property out right.

Let's say this couple decided that is what they wanted to try their hand at and they went and found a property that the tax office had with a $5K tax bill. The government has taken the property and the owner has no way of paying the bill. My fictitious family can now go and pay that bill using $5K from their $15K and have the papers on that property free and clear. Now depending on the laws of that county, they will have to give the owner some time to redeem the property. Either way, my couple wins because now the owner has to pay the interest on the amount owed to my couple. So even if they only make $500, that is better than they would get from a bank in a year's time.

Now let's say the owner cannot redeem the property and the time has lapsed for them to do so. The property then belongs 100% to my family and they can do as they please with it. I am going to say the property is worth $80K in the "as is" condition. My fictitious family owns the property free and clear, I mean out right. Let's assume the family is not interested in being landlords. I would suggest they put the property on the real estate market for $65K. This way a real estate investor can buy it fast and make money. My fictitious family will walk away with a profit of $60K by using $5K of their own money. The $5K is put back into the original savings or somewhere making a better return than a savings account.

Remember, the family left $15K in the property, so it could sell fast and the buyer would have equity to gain from the transaction also. Always make the deal a WIN-WIN situation each time you sell real estate and you will have great success. Being greedy will not get you very far in this world and people will not do business with you when they learn this about you. This scenario can be done in less than a year and it can be repeated over and over again. You can really find a property and make $5K, $10K or even $50K in less than a year.

Okay, back to my fictitious family. They made $60K. Now, they just made their money back and added $60K to their savings. Like I said before, they can go out and repeat this process over and over again using the money they earned and build their wealth that way. This could be you! You say, "Bobby I don't even have $100, where am I going to get $5K to do this"? Find 25 to 50 people to invest $100 to $250 into your new Real Estate Tax Lien Buying Company and go make it happen!

That is one of my RIVERS. I look for tax liens that I can make $5K here and $10K there. Then I can use that money to repeat the process. I am okay with the possibility of making an extra $40K or $50K a year via this RIVER. Ask yourself this question: How long could you survive without your current income on what you have stored up? You know, the money you have in the bank....401K, CD's, Merchant Money Accounts, Real Estate Income. Oh, you never heard of that? Then you need to finish reading this book!

Excusism & Excusist

Are you an Excusist? **Yep!** I made this word up. Do you practice Excusism? Do you really know if this is a word? Hopefully you are not, so continue to read.

Once you have discovered your purpose, it is your responsibly to pursue that purpose relentlessly. This will ultimately lead to success. Your situation is only a state of mind. How you think about where you are will drive you to succeed or fail. The biggest hurdle you come across on a success journey is the DREAM. Once you overcome this, the rest is a process of how long you take to pursue what you want to achieve in life.

The great thing is that most of the paths have already been walked for you. All you have to do is follow the path. When you believe in your dreams, you will be willing to make sacrifices to accomplish your dreams. If you don't believe in the dreams, you won't make the sacrifices needed and it will be obvious to successful people around you. These are people who will not be around you long. They only associate themselves with people moving in the positive direction they are moving in.

Too many times I hear people saying what they cannot or could not dream of doing. Obviously they have not been broke enough or life has just let them get by. Hear my warning. It WILL NOT be that way forever and the last thing you want to do is get caught sleeping on your post. My carnal side wanted to say something else but you all get the idea. Plain and simple, saying something is not possible is a DUMB WAY OF THINKING! It is definitely not the mind of an entrepreneur. In the mind of an entrepreneur, anything is possible. If you say you cannot do something, chances are you won't! However, if you DREAM BIG and take action to pursue that dream, you will ACHIEVE BIG!

I was watching T.V. one night and the reality show Airline was on the television. For those of you who never saw it before, it is pretty much the day to day operations with some drama of Southwest Airlines. (Which, I might add is a very great Airline). The TV cameras follow and document certain passengers as they travel with Southwest. Well, on this particular episode, there was a young lady who had missed her flight. She was all distraught and fussing at the ticket agent because she thought that she would be fired if she missed flight and did not make a really big meeting in the city where she was traveling to that day.

I mean she was saying things like, "If I don't get to this meeting, I will be fired and have no money. My daughter will have to drop out of college". You say, what is your point Bobby? Here it is and I don't know if she was playing up to the cameras or not, but if she was not, she was oh so pitiful! It is ridiculous how some of the supposed to be educated professionals of the world act when they are in a tough situation or a crisis. If the mom acts like this, most likely the daughter does to. I am warning you single folks, beware and check out the family before you marry. Look at the mama and the daddy first to see who you're marrying. Okay, I am off track a little (smiles).

First, if your job depends on you making a meeting, you probably need to look for a better firm to work for fast. Second, if being fired for something as stupid as missing a meeting will cause you to lose your home and cause your child to have to drop out of school, you really need to do something different. You need to read this book and get every tape or CD I put out. Sister, if you should happen to be reading this by some divine intervention from God, email me please. I would like to show you how to never be in that situation again.

You were bringing unnecessary financial stress on your life. Now if you're just a worry wart, don't email me, don't call me... please stay away! I know some people think if they make a scene, it will help their cause. Newsflash, if you are treating someone like dirt, they are not going to go the extra mile for you....PERIOD. Even if they could help you, 9 times out of 10, they won't because of your attitude towards them. I have seen it happen time and time again. Be nice to people, think positive and you will get more out of life.

I remember booking my flight wrong for a meeting in Las Vegas. The day of my departure, I was supposed to leave in the morning and had mistaken it for the afternoon. I got to the airport and discovered what I had done wrong. My plane had left earlier that morning. I didn't get up in the ticket agent's face and make a big scene. I did not try to make my problem their problem. I explained that I had made a mistake and what had happened. They told me how to try and fix the problem. However, the flights going out of Las Vegas were booked and I would not be able to get out of Vegas until the next day.

I know what those of you who have been to Vegas are saying. ALRIGHT! Bobby, being stuck in Vegas one more night would be great! I did not get that excited. I had planned and prepared to dodge a curve ball. I made sure I had disposable cash with me. I was able to get another room for the night. I did just that and returned to the airport the next day to fly out. I saw other people who were stuck in the airport, running around like chickens with their heads cutoff. They were fussing and cursing at each other. Three grown ladies were at the same ticket counter I was standing at and they were crying like babies. I could not believe my eyes. Note: Crying and having temper tantrums don't go very well in this world. Most people could care less about your problems because they have problems of their own.

REMEMBER THIS: Piss Poor Planning on your part does not create an emergency on someone else's part. Don't try to put your problems on someone else. Like I said, they probably can tell you about the day or night they are having or had, too. Focus on the outcome not the obstacle. Spend more time finding solutions than complaining about the problem. Complaining makes you stand still while searching for solutions moves you forward. This is why I desire so badly for you to have disposable income. So if you are ever faced with a situation like my airport issue, the money will not be an issue.

One other story is worthy of mentioning, (hold on....I have a point). There was another passenger flying on Southwest (Did I mention that I love Southwest Airlines) who assumed she could put her 2 year old on her lap. So, she took the chance and tried to fly. How many of you know that you have to pay for kids to fly? If they are breathing you have to buy a ticket! Some Airlines do allow what they call "Lap baby" travelers. Anyway, the ticket agent informed this young lady that she would have to buy another ticket. GUESS WHAT? The lady with the baby did NOT have the MONEY to pay for the extra ticket. This is all true!

I mean no money at all. She had less than an hour to get the money before boarding the airplane. I do not know how she got the money but she did and was able to fly. My point again is to have more than one income. So, when you need an extra $300 or $1000 dollars, you just take out that VISA, Master Card, American Express or Discover and handle your business. Life is much less stressful with a little extra cash. Also, you need to plan. Do your research before your travel. The last thing you want is an issue when you are trying to fly.

I learned my lesson with the Las Vegas trip. Since my thought process was good, I was able to concentrate on how I could benefit from this situation rather than focusing on the problem. In doing that, I came up with a whole new business idea that would serve a niche market. Right then and there I birthed a second Airline concept. Look for it in a city near you. I am not revealing the details of the second airline right now but you will see both airlines soon. Remember, if you DREAM IT, it can be done. In Las Vegas, I imagined something, the dream happened and now all I have to do is gain the available knowledge and follow the process to reach my goal.

Starting a business and taking control of your financial destiny is a little harder than clocking in everyday at a dead end job. If you have an MBA and all those talents sitting on your mental shelf, not being used at all; shame on YOU! Speak positive things into your life not negative. The lady who spoke that she was going to lose her job if she missed the flight was speaking negatively. What you speak and believe is usually what you will get. See things as they can be not as they are. Control that Mind!

It has been proven time and time again that if you set your mind to achieve something and pursue it relentlessly, that thing or something will soon happen....good or bad. Let's hope that you are really thinking of something good and positive. I know that it is easy to say and hard to do but it is your choice. You can stay broke and suffer all your life or put in some work now and live the life you were destined to live.

By all accounts, I was not even supposed to make it out of my hometown. I was not chosen as the most likely to succeed in high school. Yet, I started and run Technology and Media corporations with the strong potential of becoming multi-billion dollar businesses. I never went to a formal business school and I ain't got no college degrees (Yep, that's right I said AIN'T!).

I build my companies by putting people who are smarter than me around me. I hire the folks who have the college degrees for some jobs. Everybody else, I hire based on character and train for skill. I try not to harp on the academics of the thing. At my companies, we just get to it and do what has to be done to reach our goals. You should do the same. Don't get me wrong. Education is great. However, you have to have some sweat equity to go with all that theory in order to really make things happen. Theory is one thing but real life is another. Balance them both out and you will win.

Stop sitting around talking about what you can't do. Start with what you know needs to be done. Get into the routine of reminding yourself everyday of the positive things that are going to change in your life. This will allow the thoughts to become normal thoughts. Once this habit is formed, you will not allow any negative views into your brain. If the negative thoughts do get in your mind, you will recognize and reject them very quickly.

The main question is how broke do you have to be in order to change what you are doing? How many times do you need to be embarrassed about not having money before you totally change your financial life? What do you really want out of life?

The Art of Big Thinking

If you look deeper into the stories I mentioned, they all have to do with how a person thinks. Negative small thinkers receive negative results while positive BIG thinkers receive HUGE results. Remember, it does not matter where you are in life right now. You can get on the road to financial success. If you are new to this way of thinking, you have taken a giant step towards a successful financial life.

Belief is an important part of Big Thinking. Big Thinking is when you remind yourself that anything is possible. This gives you the necessary energy and motivation to reach your goals. Do not look at DREAMS as something for someone else. See yourself accomplishing those goals. Believe you can reach the goal and you will. Find someone who has done it before and follow their formula until you customize your own.

Here are my *7 Key Questions for Success*. These are some questions I would like you to ask yourself.

1. What are my Dreams and Goals?
2. What is stopping me from achieving them?
3. What do I want my Personal & Home world to be like in 5 years?
4. What do I want my Career & Business world to be like in 5 years?
5. What do I want my Social & Community world to be like in 5 years?
6. What am I willing to sacrifice to obtain my Dreams and Goals?
7. What tools and resources will I use to obtain my Dreams and Goals?

A goal is a clearly stated mission. It says to the world for you, "This is my Dream and it is what I am working on". Without goals, people go through life without knowing where they are going and/or how they will get there. I really believe Goals are as important to success as air is to life. Without goals, people die, nations and people suffer and dreams stay just dreams. Corporations plan 3 to 12 years ahead. Do not leave your future to chance. Plan at least 5 to 10 years ahead.

Remember there will be obstacles. Just take these road blocks in stride. If the highway you are traveling on is blocked, turn around and take another route. You will still reach your destination. It might just take a little longer. Just remember to enjoy the journey.

The Truth about Money

Money Is NOT the root of all evil, the PEOPLE who handle money are! Get it straight and stop making excuses for not pursuing the life you're afraid to go after. Just admit you're scared, get over it and get on with it! Money is nothing more than a tool. To get the best results with it, you need only to learn how properly to use and manage it.

If you don't learn how to properly use money, I can promise you that there is someone out there willing to show you how to in a way that best fits their interest. There are tons of scam artists in the world and the only people they get over on are the people who do not educate themselves about money.

Footnote or whatever you call it. I actually put the book down and was waiting to just put all this information on CD. Then on one late Sunday night, I was up and decided to watch a certain show. The show covers finances and usually is pretty good, but this night the host was far off base with one couple. Wait a minute, I was trying to be nice and not mention the name of the show, but I wouldn't be me if I did that.

The show I am talking about is the Suze Orman show. She had a couple on the show that was disagreeing about how to pay their bills. Well, later into the interview, Suze tells the husband about his wanting to stay in control and not being a real man. This dude was accepting it. He said he was a Pastor. Come on Bro...you're a Pastor. You are supposed to have more power than that.

Your wife should not have to go to work at night to help support the household. There are plenty of other income opportunities out there that will make more money and keep the family together. As coaches, we need to watch how we approach certain issues. The Pastor was looking for a way out, not a drama spot to increase show ratings. We as consumers also need to watch who we take our advice from because sometimes their advice does not have our best interest at heart.

My point is this. If someone is telling you that a job is what is going to get you out of debt, they are lying! You might need one to make things happen for the short haul. In this case, the wife knew that going to work during the day was counter productive. If they are that bad off, they should look into one of my favorite business industries. You know what it is, Direct Selling/Network Marketing. The wife could have found a direct selling company that she was comfortable with. There is Escape International (Aisle19), Amway, Pamper Chef, PartyLite, Tupperware, Mary Kay, Pre-Paid Legal and Avon. The wife could make more money with one of these companies than the husband and still be able to be there with her kids during the day.

Real Estate investing would be another option. Since she is at home, she has the time to do the research and pursue deals. If they don't have the money, they could team up with some other couples and make it happen that way. You have to be strategic in your thinking to create real success.

I am energized because you folks need real down to earth help. I will show you how to get the job done. Don't get me wrong here, although I disagree with what Suze had to say to the couple on that night, I still respect and support her because she has helped a lot of people. If your money is really tight, at least you and your wife can look into Ebay or something that can be done from home. Remember, business owners get more tax breaks than regular employees. That can be a good start right there.

You have to have money to operate in our culture without stress and the problems of this world. Try living without it and see how far you will get. Even when you have money, the problems still come. It is just a little easier to deal with when you have a little cash to help you out. Just try living without any money. I will see you standing on the side of the road holding a sign that says "Need Help", both in the dead heat of the summer and cold of the winter. Even those folks have a thought pattern, it is just not proper for positive success. Control the Mind!

Don't allow any Church or religious group to tell you that money is evil. If they do, they are lying to your face and most likely want to keep you in the poor house to control you. Just know the love of money is evil. I will put it this way. If that organization you belong to is not helping and encouraging you to do much better in your whole entire life (I mean Spiritually, Physically, Mentally & Financially), you should start looking for that spiritual empowerment somewhere else.

Pastors preach that you should give to the Church and yes we do have a biblical duty. However, how does someone do that if they cannot even pay their light bill? We have to change the current mindset and get folks on the right track first. We have to have serious entrepreneurial programs in our Churches so that the flock can become wealthy and support the Church. It is my belief, that everyone in the Church should have the entrepreneur's mindset. This means from the Pastor to the youngest child who can understand the process. Then, we don't have to go to the banks to build. We can raise money from within the Church. It has been done, I have seen it done.

We have to learn how to build big businesses not just mom and pop stores here and there. Just because your Pastor is selling books and tapes does not make them a true Entrepreneur. This is what I call pass through opportunities via the occupation and/or position. When you are a Pastor or a professor and you write a book, you have people to sell the book to. However, that does not make you a true Entrepreneur who can lead others. Every entrepreneur has to go through the growth process before you can teach this stuff.

Theory will only get you so far. That is why especially in a lot of Churches, the Pastor does not see it necessary to teach entrepreneurship to the flock. They are living the life and in turn the Church and the people will suffer. Give him or her $10,000, take away the 10,000 people in the Church and let's really see what happens from scratch.

I know I am going to get letters and emails stating that it is not apart of the Pastor's or Church's job to promote Entrepreneurship. I disagree. If that is the case, why are so many Pastors and Bishops promoting their own CD's, Books and Tape programs right from the pulpit? That is marketing, and isn't marketing a part of business? Isn't all of American built on the practice of Entrepreneurship? They have the 15,000 square foot house and the flock is broke as hell. What is wrong with that picture? Your leader should be able to show you exactly how to do what he or she did. They push everything else, why stray away from business?

Listen, you have every right to make as much money as you like. For some of you, that will only be $50,000 to $100,000 a year and for some it will be more. It is all dependent upon what your lifestyle goals are and whether you have a family. Now let's get something straight and clear, IF YOU HAVE A FAMILY, YOUR GOAL SHOULD NOT BE $50,000. IT SHOULD BE $5,000,000 or more. You should also be grooming your kids to become multi-millionaires. Somebody is going to have to take care of your old butt in the future. Don't you want those kids financially able to do so? So leave a legacy for your kids. Make them financially literate.

You can get more about raising rich kids in my other book: "Raising RICH Kids". Let's also get another thing straight, before I get flooded with emails and letters. Making money is not the only thing you should be working to gain in your life. Make sure to put God first, then your family, then your career. I want you to become debt free and have the right balance between your "Rivers of Wealth" and your family. Although I am not writing a book on family or God, this needed to be said. This book is about Wealth building. This chapter is about the Mindset of an Entrepreneur. See the other authors for the other topics.

My personal goals are not to accept speaking engagements or travel unless I can take my family with me some of the time. If I can't be home before the end of the night, my family will travel with me. We will spend time during the day together before I do a seminar. When I am not speaking or on the road, I work in my office Tuesday thru Thursday (10am to 3:30pm). No Mondays, Fridays, Saturdays or Sundays, if I can avoid it. So you see, the family must come before the money, but we must make money in order to have this type of lifestyle. There are too many single parents out there who cannot afford daycare. There are way too many people without health coverage. In 2009, there are over 40 million in poverty, need I say anymore?

Once you learn how to effectively handle your money, you will never have a major problem with it again. I remember when I was able to begin paying my tithes on a regular basis and was able to actually save a few hundred dollars in the bank. It felt really good.

You can do the same exact thing and more if you follow the simple plan I will lay out for you. Along the way, I will provide you with valuable resources that will assist you in your pursuit of "Rivers of Wealth". Take note and study these resources and they will teach you how to live the life you have always dreamed of having.

Continue Self-Development

Here is one last thing in this chapter before we are done. We invest in stocks, business and all sorts of other things. We study these things and learn as much as we can before putting our hard earn dollars into them. However, we fail to invest in ourselves which is the most important piece of investment property you have. Invest in success education and in things that will development your mind. Sorry but Degrees on the wall will not do it. You will have to get your hands dirty. Getting the real life information that the course provides is more important.

Buy books and magazines that prompt you to think big. Watch television that teaches you new tricks of the trade. Get ideas from these publications. If it is positive and good for your life, soak it up like a sponge and the knowledge will take you very far in life.

Control the Mind!

Chapter 6

Direct Selling/
Network Marketing
"Small Investment, Huge Potential"

What Is Direct Selling – Network Marketing

Especially now in 2009 and with the recession going on, people without disposable income should be without question running to this industry. I know you don't have the money you need to carry your dream business, so here is an alternative to get you to that point. It can be used as one income stream, a "River of Wealth".

We all have done it at least once in our lifetime. Have you ever gone to a movie or a restaurant and absolutely loved it? Then, as soon as you talked to or saw someone who you thought would love it too, you enthusiastically told them they should go see this movie or eat at this restaurant. Yep, we all have done it. Now, I have a question for you. How much did that movie studio or that restaurant pay you to tell those folks about your great experience? How long did it take before you actually got the check?

You say, *"Bobby I never got a check for that!"* I say, *"Get out of here, surely you made sure that if you did some work, you got paid!"* The point is, word of mouth advertising is the same thing as network marketing or direct selling. The only difference is that when you join an organized legal company, you get paid when people use a product or service. Most companies understand that if they can connect directly with the consumers, then they have a better chance of getting the sale. That is why you see a lot of affiliate programs and incentive programs in the marketplace today. These corporations don't mind sharing the wealth for your referral. The biggest beauty of this business is that after you make that referral, you get paid over and over again. You do the work once and get paid every month thereafter. This is called residual income and it is very real. If most of us stopped working, our pay check would stop.

If I stop getting up to talk to you on the radio (EntreWorld Today.com) or on T. V., the money stops. If most of us business owners stop going into the office and running our business, the money would soon stop coming in. If we died, what would happen to our earning potential? There are even a lot of us out here who make a decent amount of money, but the fact remains, that if we stop doing what we are doing, the money stops also.

If you have made enough to live off the interest of your money, this industry is of no use to you. Now tell me: How many people in the world are in that position? Even if you had a few million in the bank today, that would not keep up with inflation to give you a comfortable lifestyle. Sorry, but a million bucks just does not go as far as it used too.

Don't Sleep on the Industry

It makes over 30 Billion dollars in gross sales and it has so many different names. Some call it Direct Selling, Network Marketing, Multi-Level Marketing (MLM), Pyramid Scheme and a host of others things. In the past and still today, some people hear those words and run scared. They are usually the ones who really need to listen unless 'mama' or 'papa' left them a huge sum of money. Pyramid Schemes DO exist and they usually catch the idiot who is looking for a fast buck. That person is most likely NOT financially literate and is the first one to down the legit industry on any day. There are companies in this industry that are and have been publicly traded. You can not get on the United States public markets and take people for a loop for long without being exposed. Remember Enron ANYONE! They were supposed to be a straight major corporation! We will talk about this later.

Being in business is hard; it is not for the faint of heart. It will require your time, attention and it will cost you money. This is not something I read about. This is something I know from experience! So, if you have enough money to start and carry your new business for 3 to 5 years WITHOUT profit, go for it. You need not read this chapter. Move on and I hope to see you at the top. However, if you do not have at least $500 to $1500 to get the basics of your new business going and a job to take care of the bills until you make money, Network Marketing is about your only legal choice. PERIOD!

On just one certification in one city, I spent almost $700 in two weeks. I have to do business across the nation. This means that all the States, Cities and Counties that I want to do business in will require my company to spend $200 to $300 in fees alone. There are at least 400 different cities and counties my firms will do business in, try $200 times 400. That's $80,000 dollars in fees alone that we will be paying out annually. It's a good thing we can deduct those fees! Now we are not at the 400 point yet, but the number is growing rapidly. We should make a lot more than we put in, but my point is you have to have money for fees alone to operate. Permits and licenses have to be bought to operate a business.

I am going to be as straight up with you on this one as I am on everything else. This is not a pitch for you to join my company's sales force of network marketers. If you don't have a pot to piss in and are broke as a joke.... **IT IS A PITCH FOR YOU TO JOIN SOMEBODY'S NETWORK MARKETING ORGANIZATION**! Hell, you can now see AMWAY (Quixtar) advertising on CNBC. How many of you know that the owners of Amway also own the Orlando Magic basketball team? These Billionaires would not be in the business industry if it did not work.

You can also see Mary Kay along with AVON in major magazines. There is Pre-Paid Legal, Pampered Chef, Escape International (Aisle19) and a host of other legit companies in the network marking/direct selling industry. The goal is to find the company that best fits you and jump in. This industry is not new, direct selling is a business tool. **So, if you really don't have a penny to your name and need to get started somewhere, this industry is how to get off on the right foot.**

When Warren Buffet Acts

When I first started rebuilding the Jiacom direct selling organization, I made the first calls and got the first rejections. I re-structured the practices and principles. I remember calling people who actually filled out an online survey stating they were looking for a business opportunity with lower start up costs, etc., etc. but when I contacted them, "I got, not interested if it is an MLM or sales", "I have a job now", disconnected phone numbers and "Oh, I changed my mind". I hope when they changed their mind, it was over a million dollar check.

To the lady that said she had a job, my response to myself, what happens when this company fires you or lays you off? You are back at ground zero. The guy who changed his mind was nice. He must have gotten a little money and did not feel the need to work on securing the rest of his financial future. The lady, who said if it is an MLM she didn't want any part in it, is just plain old .....well, you know what I mean. She lost money trying to get a quick buck or is allowing her ignorance to cloud her judgment. I hope a money crisis never visits her door step.

Listen, when the President of the United States' campaign organization uses the MLM model for it's voter registration and growth strategy, that should tell you something. These are some of the wealthiest people in the world and you wonder why their attitude toward business is totally different. They learned it and applied it to their daily lives!

When Warren Buffet, one of the safest investors around and the World Richest man (just passed Bill Gates in 2008), buys a company in the MLM/Direct Sales industry (Pampered Chef), you have to take notice. If Mr. Buffet likes the industry, I like the industry. To become successful, do what the successful do LEGALLY! Most of you did not know who Warren Buffet was until I just mentioned his name and you still don't. That's why you have to read and what you read must be different from what you're currently reading.

Search the Internet. Warren Buffet is a very close friend of Bill Gates. I know you know who Bill Gates is. You would be crazy out of your mind if you did not take a serious look at this industry to start your financially secure future. Especially if you're totally broke right now and don't have the money to open up a franchise or start a business from scratch. In any industry (see Enron), there will be crooks who lie, cheat and steal people's money. However, in the Direct Selling industry, if YOU choose the right company, you could go a long way.

It does not matter whether the company is new or fifty years old. In this industry, you determine if you win or lose. So don't believe the hype about joining a company with experience. Some experts will tell you not to join a young company because they might not last. (Note: This is for all the small startup MLM's who are doing it right). Remember, all those old companies who have millions in revenue today and look real pretty on paper now were new companies once before. Everybody has to start somewhere. You along with your consultants can make a fortune if you keep moving forward. Big or small, old or new, people can become highly successfully via this industry. Just pick the right company at the right time like my company, Norrson International. (You know I would not be a good CEO if I did not plug my own company in my own book).

My point is, you make the decision. Check these companies out and find one that you feel comfortable with. Try two at one time, even though most would prefer you didn't, you are there to make money and secure your financial future. Don't inner recruit or sponsor, show respect to the companies you are associated with. Try a new MLM and a well established MLM and see what happens.

There are companies in this industry that are on the NYSE. You have to be legit to get listed. You can not just get on the New York Stock Exchange and be out there scheming on people. You will get a lot of jail time for that, remember Enron?

CITI financial is a part of the industry, Pre Paid legal is now backed by them. So please, do not pay attention to those folks who have the Chicken Little mindset. They are the ones saying, *"The sky is falling, this will never work"*. There are reputable companies out there giving people a real fighting chance at making some good money. Don't get into the business trying to hit homeruns, just get on base and score points. It all adds up to success for you.

There is no qualifying to be in this business industry. All you need is a little start up money with most firms and the rest is up to you. No one can require you to have a college degree. Your past experience and financial capability statements are not needed. You won't have to show your last two years of tax returns...hell if you were like me, I had not even filed because I knew I owed money. You really determine whether you succeed or not.

There is no glass ceiling, no bosses to take money out of your pocket, and no clocking in or out. You don't have to worry about your hours being cut back. A lot of you are not getting that overtime you are used to getting. How about use those overtime hours to grow your own business? You do not have to work with people you do not like. If they rub you the wrong way or you get a bad feeling about them...DON'T sponsor them! Send them on their way to make someone else miserable.

There are people who have built successful Network Marketing businesses that do not have to wake up at the crack of dawn to go to work. Their kids enjoy a healthy lifestyle and they travel at will. They are living their dreams and really enjoying life. My friend, **THIS CAN BE YOU**. You only have to make a decision to change your life for the better and relentlessly pursue it.

The network marketing companies are out here. All you have to do is choose one and go make it happen. It is not rocket science and for most Americans, it is your only option. Now, if you decide to take your chances with a good job, then that's on you. Oh...I forgot you can always play the lottery! Yah right! I will admit it. I have played the lottery here and there, but I know that I have a better chance of making millions if I find a good business to join and work it like crazy. Someone will win the lottery. It is all a numbers game, but the chances you will win are slim to none. Sorry to break that bad news to you.

Entrepreneurial Training

A great benefit of being a Network Marketer is the fact that you get so much free entrepreneurial training. You will meet and network with some very smart business owners. You find that a lot of Network Marketers have other business ventures going on and can provide you with a lot of great advice you would otherwise have to pay for. The exposure that you will get from being around people who are like minded will be priceless. You will learn and see so much more than you could ever imagine.

Most Network Marketers are a special type of people that try to keep a positive attitude for the most part. If you find one who has a bad attitude, call them out on it or report them to the company they represent. Definitely do not buy products from them or use their services. Bad attitudes should not get rewarded with sales!

The Cons of Network Marketing

As great as this business industry is, it is plagued by incorrect information and crossed communications. Most of this bad press comes from people who were so greedy that they jumped at the first opportunity that seemed great and lost their shirt. When most people are approached by a Network Marketer, they react very differently than if it was a regular business interview for a job. This is due in part to the fact that some people with no morals or self-worth used the industry model to scam people. This is evident if you do a Google search in the Internet.

You will find a great deal of Network Marketing, MLM and Direct Sales haters. If you dig deeper into these folks past and check their history status, they are not the Russell Simon, Warren Buffet, Sean "Diddy" Comb, Richard Branson, Bob Johnson, Sean "Jay Z" Carter and Michael Dell of the world. The haters and negative folks are the opposite of go-getters and have access to the Internet. Freedom of speech, go figure (smiles)! So ignore them at all costs. Negativity can not survive in success for long. These toxic people love to talk about what is wrong with something, rather than putting in the work to make that issue better. They are usually broke as hell or not far from it.

Like I said before, most of these folks are mad because they got into something they should not have gotten into and were taken to the bank. They were scammed. They saw what they thought was a quick buck and got robbed. If the business does not require work of some sort, it might be a scheme. Hear me, **NO BUSINESS VIRTUALLY RUNS ITSELF!** There are a lot of people out there who want instant gratification and they are usually the ones who get scammed.

When this happens, they think they are doing something great by telling everybody they know that the industry is worthless. Actually, they are still in network marketing. They are just not getting paid. I find that these people are barely making it in there own financial lives. So be wary of taking advice from them. I would rather take my chances on what Warren Buffet thinks. He saw fit to put $770 million into a company (Pampered Chef), so that is good enough for me. It is your choice, the advice of your broke friend or the advice of the richest man in the world!

Now don't get me wrong, I admit there are some unethical network markers in our industry. Their only concern is themselves. When you do encounter these folks, report them to your company and stay the hell away from them. Don't give them any time or support until they get their act together. We are NOT in this business to get over on people. We ARE in this business to help people change their lives.

The direct selling/network marketing industry as well as any other industry will always have some kind of negative press with it. Remember ENRON! Scammers always try to use a legit business model to get over on people. People will join your business and quit just as fast, but that is no different than a regular day with a corporation. Employees come and go depending on their wants and needs. People are going to think what they think and say what they want to say. You should not be concerned with that. Do not let others determine whether you become wealthy or not. You continue to press on.

The Pros of Network Marketing

If you are broke as a joke and do not have a solid business idea, you are really in need of some good entrepreneurial coaching. You need to be around some people who are changing their financial future with a positive outlook. You need to get with a direct selling company and become a serious network marketer. Really I should say, start getting paid for being a network marketer. You are already doing the business, yet you are not getting paid for it. STOP LEAVING MONEY ON THE TABLE!!!

Why do I say this? Well simply put, it will not cost you a lot of money to get started in the business and once you take that leap of faith, you are in business. I would not spend anymore than $500 to get with a good direct selling company. Escape International (Aisle19), Pampered Chef, Mary Kay, Quixtar, Avon, Pre-Paid Legal, and a host of many more companies allow new business owners to come into their business for less than $200.

If someone is suggesting you pay huge amounts of money to get into network marketing, get the hell away from them. They are trying to scam you...don't be dooped! Don't believe the hype! Only people who are looking for a quick buck get caught up in these types of companies and they usually lose their shirt. They did not want to do the work required to grow a real direct selling business and that is the result. This is a business that requires WORK. If you don't dedicate yourself to it, it will not yield you any returns-PERIOD! Isn't it better to spend five (5) to ten (10) years growing a solid business that will last well into your golden years. As opposed to working well into your golden years only to discover that you will continue to have to work to survive?

It is not about getting your friends to join the business anymore. Really it should have never been this way. People you don't know right now are getting laid off and downsized everyday. They are waiting for YOU to contact them with an opportunity to secure their financial future.

Look at the big three auto makers, closing dealerships, manufacturing plants and laying people off by the thousands. Surely a few of those folks will consider being in their own business via network marketing now. Sometimes it takes a lay off or bad situations at work to get them to look at this industry and that's okay. This is happening all over the world and these people will join a direct selling company. The question is will it be yours?

Now let's get down to business and find out how you and network marketing can become a good team. Most people think someone is trying to sell them on making a million bucks and because they might not be able to believe they can achieve that at that point in time, they run from the opportunity. Really, no one should be going into network marketing initially to make millions. The goal should be to get on base and make $100 to $1000 extra per month.

This is not "walk away from your job" money but it is a start. It shows you that the business model works. Just think of having an extra $1,000 per month and what that would do for your life. You could take a nice vacation, not worry about fixing the car, keep your bills paid up and invest a little every month. I know some of you are saying …"Just give me an extra $300 per month and I'm good!"

With network marketing, you CAN achieve $100 to $1000 per month in extra income. People are doing it everyday. I was on my way home one day and pulled up to this pink Cadillac. Some of you should know who the driver was. For those of you who don't, it was a lady driving the car. I can assume that either she was the owner of that car or another female was because where Cadillac usually has it's name was the name Mary Kay. Yep, now if you think about it, you have probably seen a pink Cadillac with Mary Kay on the side of it and thought nothing of it. You will see more cars like that. Mary Kay is a direct selling company and allows its consultants to earn a few different types of cars. So my point is this folks: This industry is very real and people are making money, so what are YOU waiting for?

OTHER BENEFITS of NETWORK MARKETING

Everything is already Setup

You do not have to reinvent the wheel. The company you join has most likely put everything in place for you. All you should have to do is learn the business and go out and start bringing in customers. When you start your own business, everything is on you. It will take a little bit of time for you to get the right business contacts. There will be a lot of networking and building of relationships before most will consider buying from you or joining your team. Get through the rejections and move on to the approvals. You might have to knock on one hundred (100) doors to get one (1) to open. Just keep repeating the process and wealth will soon be in your hands. The more you do the business, the better you will get and the faster it will grow.

I have learned this first hand with Jiacom and the other businesses I run. Coming out of the starting gates is always slow unless you have a lot of cash behind you. All I had was a few hundred dollars, faith and determination. I learned valuable lessons which will allow me to grow a Multi-Billion dollar direct selling company in the future.

All you need to know to start making money in your new business is the history and story of the company you're with. Learn what products or services you are going to be marketing, who your potential customers will be and a couple of good ways to approach them. Again, some folks would suggest you only go with a company that has been around for a very long time. I strongly disagree with that shortsighted view. It is like this old money, new money thing. Old money was new money once before and new money will be old money some day soon. The old Direct Selling companies were once very new and a few people got in on the ground floor. Now those folks are older and a lot RICHER.

Small risk equals small returns, big risk equals BIG returns. Don't be afraid of taking risk. You do it everyday when you get behind the wheel of your car. My best advice for choosing a direct selling company would be something you already know. Go with your gut. If it is a small company that means you can actually touch the owner. Use this advantage and have a one on one meeting with him or her. See if you see the vision and understand the process. If you do see the vision and believe in it, join the team and give it your best shot. If you don't like what you see and hear, DON'T JOIN the team!!! Find another company to work with in direct sales.

When you do join a network marketing firm, you will be surrounded by people who can coach and mentor you on ways to grow your business. Then, soon you will be doing the same thing. This is a business of leverage and duplication. You will not be in this business alone. You will be around like-minded people with like-minded goals...to become financially free. These will be people who would spend a few hours reading a book, as opposed to going to a sports bar, club or sitting in front of a T. V. all day. They will become your new circle of friends who won't look at you like you're crazy when you talk of taking trips to Hawaii and Japan. Flying on a private jet will not sound absurd to them. Floor seats at an NBA basketball game is within range and very possible to them. Season tickets to the world's best football team (Dallas Cowboys) are very achievable! Okay, I am a Cowboy's fan...so what!

People with the opposite view should NOT be in your circle of friends. Make sure you check these people out too. Doing a criminal background check is not hard. Remember, this is the world and you have some foolish unethical folks wherever you go. So don't just let anyone into your home or into your personal life. As a matter of fact, keep it business until they have proven to be business serious. Meet at coffee shops or the mall. Never let someone you just met into your home. People can pretend and act like they are with you for months.

Proceed in business relationships with caution. Ladies, watch out for the guys who dress nice and talk a good game. Make them prove that they are real and serious about business. Some of these guys know that a business card and a nice suit attract women. Don't be fooled. See how they react to the pressures of life. Then, you will see what he really is about. Any guy who is not supportive of you being in business and doing for yourself is the WRONG guy for you...PERIOD!

Men, the same goes for you. A 36-24-36 can be distracting when it comes in a nicely wrapped package. Don't be swayed by the words coming from that pretty face. Make her show and prove her business sense because at the end of the day she won't look all that good if she is broke and not trying to achieve anything.

Tax Breaks

Just getting the tax benefits available for being an entrepreneur could be a life changing benefit of joining a direct selling company. The money you save in tax breaks could be invested. This could change your life. Consult a tax professional and read <u>IRS Tax Pub 536</u>, to see all the deductions you can get for being in business. This is one way you build wealth, by understanding the tax system and using it to your gain. An individual will never get the tax benefits that a small business owner will get...PERIOD!

You can write off gas, dinners, plane trips, entertainment expenses and a host of other cost in the name of business. Now hear me well, don't try to get over on the IRS. They will eventually catch up with you and you have to pay interest or even do some jail time for a little bit of money. Do the right thing.

I always smile when I hear people complaining about paying taxes. It is the law of the land and if you are a Christian, I need not say anymore about that. Look at it this way. Regardless of how you feel about paying taxes, you could be driving on a dirt road, living without electricity, drinking dirty water and a lot more. There are people in third world countries that would love to have our tax issues. When you pay taxes for road repairs, you don't complain when that road is finished and you're driving on it. If this is you, give it up, that's negative and we don't do negative.

Besides, the tax money you pay goes to support someone's salary. The government employees need to get paid too, right? I remember hearing this man complain about having to pay $90,000 in taxes and he was really upset that he had to send that money to the IRS. I got to thinking and did some math in my head.

I figured that even if his tax bill was $90,000 flat, that meant that was only about 15% of what he had really made. He had made close to $1,000,000 in the past year that he got to keep. Now somebody tell me why would someone be complaining after making close to $1 million dollars. I would give IRS $150,000.00 if I had made that million. Obviously, this was someone who has not experienced real lack. He most likely never had to go through bankruptcy or being homeless.

Well, I have been there in LACK and HOMELESSNESS. Give me $300,000 and I will pay my tax bill and then some. Then I would flip that money and earn more. The other thing I said to myself was that this guy really did not have good advisors around him. I know there could have been something he could have spent some of that money on to keep it in his bank account.....future marketing funds, private jet transportation....something.

He should have done his homework and put the right team in place to show him where to use that extra money for future business expenses. Bottom line is, pay your taxes, get some great business advisors and know the lingo yourself. There is no reason for someone who is financially secure to have tax issues.

Residual Income

Alright, let's get down to the nitty-gritty. The best part out of all the benefits of being a network marketer is the residual income you earn and receive every month. Residual income is money you earn every month for doing work ONE TIME! You go out and sign up a customer to buy a product or use a service on a monthly basis. The parent company you have an agreement with will pay you a percentage of the business you generated every month you have that customer. Like I said before, NOT ROCKET SCIENCE!

How can they afford to do this you say? Well let's have a hypothetical distribution class here. Adidas makes a shoe for $3 dollars in another country. Then the distributor sells the shoe to a broker at a wholesale price. The broker turns right around and sells that same shoe to a wholesaler for $20 dollars. The wholesaler then sells that same shoe to a retailer (Foot Locker, Dick's Sporting Goods, Sears) for $40 dollars. The retailer then opens the box and marks that $3 dollar shoe up to $120 dollars. You and I walk into the store and buy it at the marked up price.

Direct Selling companies have figured out how to go directly to the manufacturer to buy products and services. They then set up (Create an Opportunity) a group of people in their own business to take that product or service directly to you and me the consumer. Those people are referred to as the NETWORK who MARKETS these products and services. Hence the term Network Marketers is what they are called. Because we deal directly with the consumer, the term DIRECT SELLING is used.

Some of the money saved from not having to go from wholesaler to retailer is passed to the consultant as residual income. Now with the power of the Internet, it is even easier to build a business in this industry.

The monies that come back to the consultants differ from company to company. This is still the only industry that allows you to earn what you are really worth without a glass ceiling. You can earn as much or as little as you would like. In a nutshell, the direct selling companies pay you to market to potential customer's verses going the regular media and distribution routes with all their monies. Hands down, "Word-of Mouth" advertising has always been the best type of advertising around.

You get to Contribute

You help others while helping yourself. This is called contributing or giving back. This is a must if you are going to really enjoy your wealth and abundance. When you understand that it is not all about the money and start helping people when you get wealth. Life will flow much easier for you. Have you ever wondered why some people you know who have a great deal of money also have the worst type of attitude? They are always in the news for something stupid they did. You say to yourself, *"Man if that was me and I had all that money, I would never act like that. I would never do that, how could they do something like that with ALL that money they have?"*

Well most of the time there is something in their lives they hate or have yet to get a handle on. Regardless of how much money they have made, they still wind up in a bad situation. You have to be as close to being well rounded in all areas of your life as possible to be able to monitor yourself. When you can contribute and give from the heart, that's the real wealth and it will lead to more and more financial abundance. Even if you only have time, give of that. Doing something as simple as giving a $20 bill to help the lady with kids in the grocery store. Motivating someone who has fallen into a depression pit is a way to give back. Don't wait until you have gained wealth to start. Start now and start today!

Be Your Own Boss (Eventually)

Don't quit your day job just yet. This business requires work and will take some time to grow. When I say it takes some time to grow. I mean two (2) to five (5) years. This depends on how fast you want to grow and how much time you decide to put into growing the business. Now compare two (2) to five (5) years to twenty (20) to thirty five (35) years at someone else's business who only pays you when you clock in and hopes they can replace you without having to give you a check for the rest of your life.

Once you grow the business and the business exceeds your day job monthly check you can consider leaving. Only leave if you are sure you are going to work the business more and you HAVE a good savings. You have to determine what you need to live off of for at least two years. When you have that secure amount in the bank along with residual income...you should be good.

That residual income should be at least $5,000 per month with about two years of your current salary in the bank. Your living expenses can not go up and you really have to grow your business even more. Within those two years, you should be able to do some other business deals, i.e., flip a property or two and make another $10,000 to $50,000. The goal should be to use the network marketing business to gain the freedom and finances to create other "Rivers of Wealth" or else you will find yourself back working for someone. Clocking in and clocking out...taking thirty minutes lunches when your employer feels like giving you one.

I know there are a lot of skeptics out there who say that you can not really make large amounts of residual income. I am here to prove them wrong. Here is some homework. Choose any PUBLICLY TRADED direct selling company (Pre-Paid Legal, Avon, and Mary Kay) get their SEC file and there should be a section with the average consultant commission pay. Study it and tell me if there are not some people out there making decent money. Remember the goal should not be for you to make a million bucks. Start off slow and grow. Use all the experience you gain and connections to get into other business deals. This is how you will create true wealth.

In the Mary Kay newsletters, they even share what their top performers are making. Notice I said TOP performers. The people who grabbed the bull by horns and made it go the way they wanted it to go. If the company is publicly traded, the information is free to read by the public. Do your own research and you will see the truth.

Go make it Happen!

Norrson
Media Group

"The best thing about the future is that it only comes one day at a time."

Abraham Lincoln

Chapter 7

CREDIT & REAL ESTATE

"Credit + Real Estate = Wealth"

The World of Credit

I cannot stress this point enough. Having damn near perfect credit IS A MUST! In order to really take full advantage of what our world has to offer, you HAVE to have your credit in order. If you do not, you will suffer the consequences. It is that plain and simple. Life will be so much fun with great credit. You will be able to get better rates on the few items you do finance. When you decide to start that dream business, you will be able to go to the bank and get a credit line to carry the business. You will be able to get a new car when your current one is ready to give out.

When you have bad credit, companies can legally discriminate against you. You will only be offered the scraps when you have bad credit. I know you all have seen the offers ("Fix your Credit $39) on the side of the road. NEWS FLASH! You can fix your own credit. You do not need anyone to fix your credit. You broke your credit, so fix it! Most of the time the only thing these folks do is go in and dispute everything on your credit report. Once the companies you owe figure this out, they are going to report your debt right back to the credit reporting agency. They can provide a temporary fix to get you to buy what they want you to buy, then it's back to the same problem. If you owe the debt, figure out how you are going to get it off your credit for good. Remember this is something you can do yourself. There are some great folks out there who can help you with your credit. However, I believe that this is a task you should handle yourself. Men, we should know credit like we know sports. Ladies, you should know credit like you know your favorite love story. Once again, if you do not master this element of life you will suffer the consequences.

It is very important to have your credit straight because that is how the world views you. Like I said in a previous chapter, everyone from the employer to your local hospital is checking your credit today. Everybody wants to see your payment history to try and determine if you are going to pay them. Banks use the score to determine how much money they are going to lend you, at what rate they will lend it to you or whether they should pass on you altogether.

Growing up, no one discussed credit with me and it cost me millions of dollars. Had I known then what I know now...(remember that saying?), I would have been a lot better steward of my credit and therefore been able to move on a lot more deals and made a hell of a lot more money! That is why it is important to freeze your kid's credit and ensure that they fully understand how it works. They need to know how to protect and use it. You will be doing them a huge favor. The credit score is now a part of everyone's financial report card. You thought when you got out of school the report cards were over. Nope, we are all still getting graded by the world.

Your credit score or FICO score can range from 300 to 850 with 300 being the lowest score. It is 2009 now and 600 to 700 used to be considered doing pretty good. Now you need at least a 750 score to get decent deal and good interest rate. Remember after that deal, your score will go down until some on-time payments show up in the credit system.

An 800 credit score will be great; if you can get there. Your life will be much easier as far as money and credit are concerned. Just don't go out and max the credit out after you get it to the 800 level. Financers have tightened their lending belts and made it much harder to get certain things. My solution to this is just not to finance anything. Beat them at their own game. If they don't want to work with you, don't buy from them.

We need to stop buying things on credit anyway. That is why all of us are in the situation we are in now. Finance the car if you have to and even the house. The rest of the stuff, buy with cash. If you do not have the cash, DO NOT finance anything! Wait until you have the cash to purchase the product or service you desire. <u>The problem buying with only cash is that we as a people want everything NOW. The instant gratification syndrome is KILLING US.</u>

I have seen people with a 500 credit score get in a brand new home, but guess what...the interest rate was out of this world. Don't get so desperate that you do any kind of deal just because you think it is the American Dream. If you have to stay in that apartment one more year, then so be it. At least when you go to the negotiating table you will have some leverage. The last thing you want to happen is that you squeezed by a broker and get into a home that you can not really afford and the bottom drops out. Remember in an earlier chapter, we talked about the *Curve Balls* of Life?

Just when you don't expect it, something can happen that requires your money to go somewhere else. You find yourself 3 months behind in the mortgage or that car note and there it is....your credit gets shot and you have to start all over again. So, if you have 3 to 6 months worth of living expenses in the bank, DO NOT BUY A NEW HOME! Wait until your money is right and then the process will be much more enjoyable. The banks and mortgage companies will try to tell you different. They want you to get in that house but not because they care about your well-being. Most of them could care less if you become financially secure. They want that big commission check that comes to them after you sign your name on that dotted line.

You make them work for you and you stay in control of the situation. Your CREDIT is on the line here....stay focused. Listen, I don't care how much you Prayed over it. If your money is not right, God does not want you to put yourself in a worse position than you are already in right now. Remember to weigh the <u>WANTS</u> against the <u>NEEDS</u> and hopefully that will help you make the right decision. Making a commitment in an emotional state, like being in that brand new home and knowing you have never had the pleasure of being in a new home can make you sign on that line right then. I know, I did it and lost $30,000 and regret it to this day.

I know what I am talking about. I saw you. The agent and loan officer were telling you the home could be yours in a month or two. Man, you are pre-approved. All you have to do is turn in some paperwork and it is a done deal. DON'T DO IT. Think about it. If you are pre-approved, then the opportunity is not going anywhere. The longer you wait, the better the deal gets. The sales agent is not going to like it but who is taking on the debt them or you? Is that agent going to lend you some money when you cannot make the mortgage payment? This economy puts you in control. There are many real estate deals at every turn. Don't be that person whose home I am buying because it is in foreclosure or those taxes are now due. If I pay them, you will have to pay me to get it back with interest.

Now that I have beaten you up on that, there is one and only one reason that I would say forget what I just said. That is if you come across a deal that will put $20,000 or more in equity into your pockets fast. Then I say go for it and manage your budget like a mad man. It is not worth it if you are only going to get $5,000 or $10,000. That money will be sucked up in things you did not see before you bought the home, unless it is a new home. So for new homes, the deal has to give you at least $10,000 and for an old home, you need to profit at least $20,000 period.

Personal Credit

If you don't already know the status of your personal credit, the FIRST thing you need to do is get a copy of your report from the three personal credit reporting agencies. These agencies are **www.experian.com**, **www.transunion.com** & **www.equifax.com**. You can get a FREE copy of your credit report from each agency without a credit score once a year from **www.annualcreditreport.com**.

When you pull your own credit, it does not damage your credit score. When ANYONE else pulls your credit, it HURTS your score. Your score will drop some points. ALWAYS pull your own credit report and score. This way you know what you are working with before you go to buy an item or do a deal.

WARNING: Watch out for these folks who make their website look like the real credit reporting agency but are fakes. There are a lot of websites that are fakes. If you are not paying attention to the URL and/or Website address, you will be duped. The best way to get to the legit websites as it pertains to credit and money are from the FTC: **www.ftc.gov** or your State Attorney General Office website. Each one of the three personal credit agencies can provide you with a credit score. The middle number is usually what lenders take into consideration. For example: Let's say you have a 603 score with Experian, a 659 with TransUnion and a 722 with Equifax. Your middle score will be 659 and that is what lenders will use to determine what you will or will not get. You can also get your credit report and score by going to: **www.myFICO.com**.

I recommend staying away from the department store credit cards. They hurt your score more than they help it. You get it all the time, "Save an Extra 10% when you apply for this credit"....JUST SAY NO and keep it moving. That little 10% will hit your credit score and bring it down. You should be paying cash for those items anyway. If you don't have the cash, you don't need the item. If you need a new Heating and AC unit, credit is okay...this will add to the value of your home. The new hot red dress will make you look good for only one night....you choose. The rims on that brand new car are not such a wise choice either.

If you really want the status of having a credit line, get it from a bank. This way when you go to buy a home or investment property, the lender sees that you have credit that is in good standing with a bank. This carries more weight than a department store credit card. Three to five open credit lines is all you need to do business in the world. Two (2) credit cards, One (1) Gas Card, One (1) Bank Loan and One (1) Mortgage payment showing up on your credit report.

Notice, I did not mention a car note. Even though the car note will show up on your credit report, I do not think you should carry a car note for long. I recommend doing enough deals to buy your car out right. I must admit, that I will have my company get my dream car but it will not be on my personal side of the house. This way, I can write it off on my business taxes and it will not be a car I drive all the time.

My philosophy is buy necessity and lease luxury via a business. Luxury changes with the wind so you don't want to get stuck in something you can not get out of. Have your business lease your dream car and even a dream home and change up ever two or three years. That is one of the benefits of being an entrepreneur. Just like taxes, you really need to know this credit score game and there are a lot more companies besides the ones listed that capture data on you and make credit profiles. Get as many books on the subject as you can and read them at least three times. Once you master the credit game, you will be a force to be reckoned with in this world.

Business Credit

To learn more about business credit, you can visit **Dun and Bradstreet** at **www.dandb.com**. I must say, I really do not care for the sales tactics the reps at Dun and Bradstreet use; they try to hard sell you when they get your business information. I usually get a call saying someone has tried to access my credit profile and they want to show me how to build that credit profile for $500. Please, if the company wants to do business with me, they are going to do business with me. They can call me directly and I will provide them with the necessary trade references to verify my business credit. The only reason I even have a DUNS number, as it is often called, is because the Federal government requires it to become a federal vendor.

So, note to DandB: Get a grip on your sales' tactics as they are annoying. When you get a DUNS number and the sales people call you trying to sell you some kind of package, tell them you are not interested and hang up the phone. If they persist, write a letter to the FTC and put it on record. Some companies teach their sales reps not to take no for an answer. Small businesses should not be spending money on a credit profile. Just pay your bills on time and your profile will be just fine. Contact DandB after you get some trade references and some revenue.

Also, most businesses don't even want a DUNS number. They prefer to have your EIN or Employer Identification number. You get this for free from the IRS website at: **www.irs.gov**. You **DON'T** have to pay a lawyer $250 to do this for you. You can go do it yourself. Listen to some of my radio shows on my website at: **www.bobbynorrson.com.** I explain all the ways to set up your business and build business credit, without spending a ton of money. In the old days, people needed to hire professionals to do this work for them. Now you can do it yourself and save the money to invest into your new business.

Another really great source to get all kinds of information from is Bankrate, **www.bankrate.com**. This website has a ton of great information on it. I recommend subscribing to it...IT IS FREE and you will see what I am talking about. Bottom line, if you do not have to use credit, DON'T....it is too easy to get trapped like a wild animal and the companies will ride you like you stole something until they get the money you owe them. If you do decide that you need business credit, never use more than half of your balance...this will show that you are not maxed out on your cards and your score will reflect this as good.

We live in a world where all the companies want you to slide that card. Don't get caught up in the fast pace of things. Remember computers are doing the work and they

WILL fail at times, so have some CASH in your pocket just in case. Ladies, you need to also keep at least $20 to $50 cash on yourself. That store you're shopping at might have a satellite problem and will not be able to process your credit or debit card.

Technology is great, but it fails and you have to be prepared for it. Since we are talking about cards and credit, I have to mention the debit cards and the fees banks are charging. I know it has happened to you. You use that debit card with a few dollars in the account at your local Subway. Then, when you get your bank statement you discover that you were charged $35 for not having enough funds in your account to cover the purchase. That sandwich just cost you $40 dollars. This happened to me all the time. Now, I just pull all the cash out of the bank. The system will charge your card, then reverse it and charge it later. This process can easily cause an insufficient funds charge to your account. However, if we have enough money in the bank, this would not be a problem.

You know you checked your account that morning before you went off to work. How could this happen? Well, basically, you forgot about another purchase you made and the bank statement did not show it. Once again, now you paid $40 for a sandwich you could have made at home. Remember, when you use your debit card, sometimes it will cycle in your account day and not process for a few more days if you did not use the PIN number for the transaction.

This is bad for you, because it registers like a bounced check. However, banks love it when this happens. It is a very easy way to make a lot of money. Think about it, if 100,000 people make this mistake per month at $35 a pop....that is $3.5 million dollars the bank is making without even trying. On top of that, they make a report out on you and when you go to open up an account, they review this to see if you're worthy of their time. Remember, the overdraft fees are treated just like bounced checks. If you get too many of them, the bank will close your account and stack even more fees on top of that. This can find its way on to your credit report and cause more problems.

There is a solution to this problem. I know some banks are going to hate me for this, but so what. When your check gets deposited into your bank account, since you have already done your bills and you know what you need to pay for the month. Go to the bank and take out what you need for bills and other stuff. Leave in the account enough to cover fees and savings. This could be $50 or $200 or whatever you choose. Banks are still making money on the little you have left in the bank account.

Now that you have all the money out you need, put the debit card up on the shelf until you need it next month! Don't pick it up for convenience or anything like that...PUT THE CARD UP! Now you don't have to worry about using the card and getting overdraft fees. I remember one time I got hit with seven overdraft fees in one month. That was like $245 that I needed, but the bank got it as soon as my check was deposited. This happened to me on many other occasions until I changed my habits and started putting the card up as soon as I took the money out of the bank. Stop throwing money away and you will build wealth much faster, I guarantee it. You will also be saving your credit!

Real Estate Investing

Now, if you were to ask me what was the best way to build wealth in a secure way, my first suggestion would be real estate investing. It is the best way, especially now in 2009, while the housing market and mortgage crisis is going on. You can go buy a home that has $30 to $100 thousand equity in it and that would be a huge start for you on your path to building wealth. People are doing that right now. Your credit does have to be pretty good and you will need some money.

However, I don't think now is the time to be sticking yourself out there on a limb either. Sales are much slower now, so be careful. Only invest in real estate if you have the means to pay for the property when you buy it. It is very easy to get into a nice piece of property. Having the money to cover that monthly note is the key. So do your homework and make sure all your ducks are in a row before you start.

As I mentioned in an earlier chapter, I did my first real estate investment deal with $100 down and made close to $25,000. I did this while having a day job with a family. Image how good I felt doing that deal and going into work. I will tell you, it felt great to know that I had just increased my earnings by $25,000 and did not have to work one hour of overtime to do it. The deal was done in less than 60 days. How much overtime would you need to work to earn $25,000?

YOU can do the same thing! After you have gotten your money together like we talked about and you know where your credit is, you can start preparing to buy your first investment property. This could be a property that you live in or lease out and let someone else help you pay the mortgage. Once you do the first deal, repeat the process at least once per year. You will be very wealthy by the time you get ready to retire if you don't retire sooner.

My goal, for example is to buy and/or build new apartments and sit on them for a few years. Then I will sell them to the highest bidder and repeat the process. By doing this about 10 or 20 times...I could easily put $1 million in the bank cash! Once again, you can do the same thing, even if you have to partner up with a few people. Get together and make some deals happen to build wealth.

If you want to invest in real estate, get every book on the subject that you can and read them at least three times. Join your local real estate investing association and build relationships, then watch your small business will grow. Remember, building wealth is not hard, it just takes time.

The discipline and determination you need to maintain it can sometimes be challenging. However, the technical process of success has already been laid out. All you have to do is stay the course. Even if you are one day out of bankruptcy, you can still do it. Knowledge is the true King......not money....not stuff, so get that knowledge and build wealth!

See you at the TOP!

Chapter 8

Doing Business
with the Government

"Small or Big business, Billions are available"

Red Tape City: Got Scissors?

A lot of current and future entrepreneurs do not even want to think about trying to do business with the government. The first thing that comes to mind is all the RED TAPE they will have to deal with to get to the first successful bid. My feeling is just get a large pair of scissors and start cutting away. Take it one day at a time and eventually you will reach the finish line. Really, once you learn the processes, it is not all that bad. Yes, there are a lot of websites, a lot of rules and regulations to deal with. Yes, it can become overwhelming. With that said; there is a ton of help there for you as a business owner. This assistance is also FREE!

So don't be afraid to jump right in and get a piece of that pie. The government is especially looking to help Women Owned Businesses, Minority Owned Businesses, Veteran Owned Businesses and Service Disabled Veteran Owned Businesses. There are laws that state that a certain amount of bids be set-a-side for small business concerns. Why are you not getting your share of the pie?

What are the Opportunities?

You can sell everything from socks to weapons to the federal government. In 2006, the Federal government had over $340 Billion to spend with small businesses. In 2007, the Federal government had over $378 Billion to spend with small businesses.

<u>Note:</u> It does not matter what type of shape the economy is in, the government spends money. Need I remind you of all those bailouts to the major corporations?

Here are the exact numbers.

Federal Government Goaling Report 2006: Total Small Business Eligible Dollars was **$340,212,001,110.44**. Don't believe me, look at it for yourself. Visit this link.

http://www.fpdsng.com/downloads/top_requests/FPD SNG_SB_Goaling_FY_2006.pdf

Federal Government Goaling Report 2007: Total Small Business Eligible Dollars was **$378,507,701,469.81**. Don't believe this either. Okay here is that link.

http://www.fpdsng.com/downloads/top_requests/FPD SNG_SB_Goaling_FY_2007.pdf

The 2008 Goaling Report will be out in early 2010. Listen to my radio show; I will get you the numbers as soon as I get them.

Here is the deal, if you are a small business, especially Women, Minority or Veteran Owned. There has never been a better time to learn how to do business with the federal government. Like I said before, there are new changes and laws that make it even easier for you to do business with the government. Don't worry about not knowing everything about the process today, start now and take baby steps to winning bids. If you can accept credit and debit cards, that is even better!

Even though I am concentrating on the Federal government, basically the same rules apply for State, County and City government. As you know, when you get to State, County and City government, everybody has their process. Just determine who you want to do business with and go after it. Oh don't worry, you will not need a lot of money to get started. For some small business owners, their first revenue was a federal contract. My technology and media firms have not won any bids as of the writing of this book. However, we are looking for solicitations everyday. One day, we will find and bid on the perfect contract.

What is Micro-Purchasing?

In addition to government contracting, there is another great opportunity that is not mentioned much in conversations when talking about doing business with the government. That secret opportunity is called "**Micro-Purchasing**" and it is a great way to do business with the government and get paid fast. This is credit card buying from the government agencies that usually have a spending limit of $2,500. So, if your small business does not accept credit cards, maybe you should start accepting them ASAP!

Billions are spend every year just using government credit cards. Do not be left out of this pool. Instead of me trying to put all the spending numbers in my book, simply go to the

Federal Procurement website and download the government FY 2007 Federal Procurement Report yourself. The website is www.fpdsng.com. You can find all the spending reports at the bottom left hand side of the webpage.

How do I register my Small Business?

Any business wishing to do business with the federal government is required to register the business in the Central Contractor Registration (CCR) system. This is the main database for government contractors. This is not an easy process and it will take preparation and time. However, there should be a step by step guide on the website to help you along. The website address is **www.ccr.gov**.

How do I find my Customers?

To figure out which government agency and/or agencies are going to be your customers just look around to see who needs your products and services. Create your own database and then get the names and email addresses of the procurement offices for that agency and make contact. Make contact after you are ready to sell your product or service. Most businesses that do business with the government have what is called a "Capabilities Statement". Basically, this is a one sheet document that has the most important information about your company on it. Business owners email this document to the procurement officers as a marketing piece.

Another way to get an idea of who is buying what and what they are paying for products and/or services is to visit **www.fbo.gov**. Do a search for awards and you will be able to see exactly what the agencies have been asking and paying for in the federal marketplace.

Who will help me?

You DO NOT have to pay for any assistance in doing business with the federal government. I repeat. You DO NOT have to pay for any assistance in doing business with the federal government! When you get registered in CCR.gov, you are going to start receiving emails from companies who have gone into the database and pulled your information, **Yep**, your email address also. I suggest you set up an email such as info@yourcompanyname.com and use that as your default email. That way, if you get too much spam you can close it and setup a new one. NOTE: This is not also bad, I have gotten some good emails from companies I plan to do business with. So leave the lines of communication open but just watch out for the schemers.

There are some reputable companies out there that can help you with your federal bids but why pay for something that is FREE from the government. The federal government has **Procurement Technical Assistance Centers (PTAC)** all across the nation that provides FREE assistance to small businesses who desire to do business with them. All you have to do is call and set up the meeting. Their website address is **www.aptac-us.org.**

What is Sub-Contracting?

Doing business with the federal government doesn't always mean you have to work directly with the government agency. Becoming a Sub-Contractor is the alternate way to still be in the game making money. A lot of contracts require the Prime contractor to have Women, Minority or

Veteran Owned businesses attached to their proposals. This way everyone wins. Becoming a Sub-Contractor until your business is strong enough to become a Prime contractor is not a bad move at all.

What is a Prime Contractor?

A Prime contractor is the main company that actually wins the contract with the Federal government for a product or service. For example, I know all of the Advertising and Marketing agencies that have the advertising contracts for certain government agencies right now. One company has a $1.3 Billion contract for the US Army advertising campaign.

My company can not financially or staffing wise handle a contract that big. So, we would look to get small pieces of that contract if the main company would allow it. It would mean marketing to the Prime contractor and hoping that a business relationship could come out of the talks. Now eventually my company will be able to handle that contract, as a matter of fact we are preparing to go after that $1.3 Billion contract when it comes open again.

Some Prime contractors are not going to pay you any attention. Don't worry about that, just find another company that is willing to do business with you and go get those Federal dollars. Sooner or later your company will be the Prime contractor if you stay the course.

What are the Rules and Regulations?

There are plenty of federal contracting rules and regulations. I am not going to go in depth on this topic.

Learn them as you go. Just remember this is the federal government and if you lie, cheat and/or steal eventually someone will catch up to you. Yo will do jail time and it is not worth it. DO NOT try to get over on the federal government. The extra money you will get is not worth jail time. DON'T be GREEDY! When you bid on contracts, the rules and regulations will be spelled out to you, just follow them to the letter. If you feel you have been cheated or mislead, then there is a special office setup to assist you.

What is OSDBU?

The Small Business Act as amended by Public Law 95-507 established the Office of Small and Disadvantaged Business (OSDBU). The Director of the OSDBU is the primary advocate within each Federal Executive Agency responsible for promoting the maximum practicable use of all designated small business categories within the Federal Acquisition process.

The Office of Small and Disadvantaged Business Utilization (OSDBU) is charged with ensuring that each Federal government agency and their large prime vendors comply with federal laws, regulations and policies. This is to include small business concerns as sources for goods and services as prime contractors and subcontractors.

Some Federal government departments and entities may have offices in their organizations that are not designated as OSDBU but have similar responsibilities. The goal of the OSBDU and each of these offices is to advocate for and manage the small business utilization programs for their organization. To find a complete listing of Federal government departments and OSBDU offices visit http://www.osdbu.gov/offices.html.

I know it might seem overwhelming, but you can do this. Do not leave this money on the ground. Now let's talk about two other opportunities that are still not talked about enough as a viable business opportunity with the federal government. It kills me that we do not talk about this in schools. Do we not want our youth to know this stuff so that they can become financially independent?

SBIR & STTR – www.sbir.gov

The U.S. Small Business Administration (SBA) Office of Technology administers the **Small Business Innovation Research (SBIR)** Program and the **Small Business Technology Transfer (STTR)** Program. Through these two programs, the SBA ensures that the nation's small, high-tech, innovative businesses are a significant part of the federal government's research and development efforts.

There are eleven Federal departments that participate in the SBIR program. Five departments participate in the STTR program awarding $2 billion to small high-tech businesses. The U.S National Science Foundation administers the SBIR.GOV site on behalf of the federal government. Everything you need to know about these programs is on that website. Let's say you would like to be an entrepreneur but you do not know exactly what type of business you would like to start. You have not yet defined what you are really passionate about or your passion will not generate enough money to live off of right now. Maybe you have tried a few businesses and none of them really worked out. Now you are looking for something else to do in business. When I first found out about the SBIR and STTR programs, I fell in love with the concept. I wish I had known about the programs a long time ago. Our government has to always be innovating and making better products. Basically, these programs are the wish list of the federal government looking for small businesses to do research, create and sell them the new products.

SBIR/STTR Example:

I once saw a SBIR solicitation for a special lubricate to put on the wings of an aircraft to prevent icing. The SBIR program has awards in three stages. Stage one gives you up $100,000 to do the research. Stage two provides you with up to $750,000 to get a working prototype and stage three becomes the sales stage of the program. If the product is suitable, the federal government may purchase it from your small business. In addition to selling the product to the federal government, your small business will be able to sell that same product to the commercial marketplace.

This is a great way to start a successful business. Knowing who your customer will be out of the gate is a great way to grow. Remember, if our government uses the product, most likely the commercial marketplace will also. To see some of the solicitations, visit the SBIR website at www.sbir.gov.

Learn this information and pass it along to your kids. They will love you for it. Remember, there are FREE Federal and State resources to help you start and grow your business. Use THEM!

Norrson
Media Group

"Today the greatest single source of wealth is between your ears."

Brian Tracy

Don't Quit

When things go wrong, as they sometimes will,
When the road you're trudging seems all uphill,
When the funds are low and the debts are high,
And you want to smile, but you have to sigh,
When care is pressing you down a bit
Rest if you must, but don't you quit.

Life is queer with its twists and its turns,
As everyone of us sometimes learns,
And many a failure turns about
When they might have won, had they stuck it out.
Don't give up though the pace seems slow,
You may succeed with another blow.

Often the goal is nearer than,
It seems to a faint and faltering man,
Often the struggler has given up
When he might have captured the victor's cup;
And he learned too late when the night came down,
How close he was to the golden crown.

Success is failure turned inside out
The silver tint of the clouds of doubt
And you never can tell how close you are,
It may be near when it seems so far;
So stick to the fight when you're hardest hit,
It's when things seem worst that you must not quit!

Anonymous

Norrson
Media Group

"You can have everything in life you want if you will just help enough other people get what they want."

Zig Ziglar

Resources

Here are some websites that I think will help you along the way as you start, grow and maintain your businesses. The websites will lead to many more websites. Don't forget to read and subscribe to magazines that focus on wealth building, business and money. So, start to compile your own resources list that you can refer back to from time to time.

Minority Supplier Diversity – **www.msdc.org**

Security and Exchange Commission – **www.sec.gov**

Internal Revenue Service - **www.irs.gov**

Small Business Administration - **www.sba.gov**

Federal Trade Commission - **www.ftc.gov**

Federal Communications Commission - **www.fcc.gov**

Business Resources - **www.business.gov**

Federal Procurement Data System (FPDS)
www.fpds.gov

Grants.gov - **www.grants.gov**

Small Business Innovation Research (SBIR)
Small Business Technology Transfer (STTR)
www.sbir.gov

National Minority Supplier Development Council
www.nmsdc.org

www.USA.gov

www.USAjobs.gov

www.Ed.gov

www.VA.gov

www.VetBiz.gov